Reading Development
and Cohesion

Reading Development and Cohesion

L. John Chapman
Sub-Dean, Faculty of Educational Studies
The Open University

HEINEMANN EDUCATIONAL BOOKS
London and Exeter (NH)

Heinemann Educational Books Ltd
22 Bedford Square, London WC1B 3HH

Heinemann Educational Books Inc
4 Front Street, Exeter, New Hampshire 03833, USA

LONDON   EDINBURGH   MELBOURNE   AUCKLAND
HONG KONG   SINGAPORE   KUALA LUMPUR   NEW DELHI
IBADAN   NAIROBI   JOHANNESBURG
EXETER (NH)   KINGSTON   PORT OF SPAIN

©L. John Chapman 1983
First published 1983

Chapman, L. John
  Reading development and cohesion.
  1. Reading
  I. Title
  428.4'3   LB1050
  ISBN 0-435-10161-7

Photoset in 10 on 12 point Melior
by GMGraphics, Harrow-on-the-Hill, Middlesex.
Printed and bound in Great Britain by
Biddles Ltd., Guildford and King's Lynn

Contents

To the women in my life,
 Mary, Elizabeth and Gillian

List of Figures

List of Tables

Preface

This book has been written to help teachers in one of their most important tasks, namely the teaching of reading. Much has been written already about this topic; the past decade however, has witnessed some important advances in our knowledge of reading, and of language in particular.

The decade has also seen changes in society which have been reflected in our schools and the demands made on them. Uppermost among these expectations is the requirement for all children to be proficient in the skills of reading and writing. This, you may protest, has always been so, but perhaps what has not been appreciated is the subtle way in which the level of proficiency being anticipated by society has also changed. The expectation is that the standard of reading and writing for all children will be more or less at the level acquired by erstwhile grammar school pupils.

One of the implications of the changes and the demands that go with them is that reading now has to be conceived in a much wider context than it has been. As such, it must become the concern of all the teaching force, for the task facing schools is of such a magnitude that it will require the combined efforts of primary, middle and secondary school teachers to achieve the desired results.

Before this is dismissed as unwarranted exaggeration we should stop to consider the effects of schools not achieving the goal of literacy for all to higher standards. If society's demands, reflected in the statements of politicians (for example, the very recent 'core curriculum proposals'), are not met, disillusion with education will follow and this, in turn, must reflect on teachers and on the status of their profession in society.

The intention of this book, therefore, is to show ways in which the teaching of reading, once mainly the concern of the infant school, is now seen to involve all teachers, since the concept of reading has so greatly expanded over the past two decades. It is hoped that in recognising this, teachers in middle and secondary schools will begin to see how they might develop teaching strategies that will go some way to achieving the results now being expected. The book assumes a minimum level of linguistic knowledge and is written so that those to whom the ideas are new can readily understand them. For those who have some prior knowledge and wish to learn more, suggestions for further reading have been included in the reference section at the end of the book. It should be emphasised that the reader is not expected to follow up these references for an understanding of the topics being advanced; they are to extend them for the reader already familiar with them.

A word about technical terms will not come amiss at this point, for, at the many meetings the author has attended for teachers of reading, it has been found that there is an initial stage during which terms that are new to the audience are commented upon deprecatingly as jargon, but as those same terms become familiar they become part of the teachers' professional vocabulary so that what was once despised jargon becomes everyday technical vocabulary. In the pages that follow some technical terms are used but they have been kept to a minimum, and when they are introduced they have been explained and illustrations provided.

The book falls into three sections. The first part (Chapters 1–3) shows that reading is best understood in the context of language; as such it requires an expansion of the concept we have of reading.

To read we need a text and one of the ways of showing that a text is a text rather than a haphazard collection of sentences is to look at ways in which it holds together, to see how cohesive it is. The second part of the book (Chapters 4–7), therefore, introduces the five groups of cohesive ties that can be found in texts and provide the mechanics of cohesion. Although these are quite straightforward, some of the detail of their usage in school texts can be complex. If you want more advanced knowledge, or are unsure, it is recommended that you have a copy of Halliday and Hasan's (1976) book *Cohesion in English* by you as a reference as I only provide an introduction. Chapter 8 deals with cloze, a technique for probing language awareness, and Chapter 9 summarises and extends some of the previous chapters in terms of comprehending.

As far as I know this is the first attempt to communicate some of these ideas to teachers and as with most first attempts will have many flaws, for which I apologise. I hope, however, that teachers will develop the ideas in their classrooms and if possible let me know of their findings.

Acknowledgements

Many colleagues and friends have contributed to the development of the thoughts presented in this book and it is impossible to name them all. It is best, therefore, to note the institutions where I have worked and mention the few who have been directly involved with the later stages of this book.

My interest in language and the teaching of reading originated in my work for many years as a teacher and Headmaster in schools in the Midlands. After a few years in teacher education at Dudley College of Education, I joined the staff of the Open University and worked on language and reading courses for teachers.

I wish to acknowledge with thanks the very helpful comments on an earlier draft by members of the Language Development Course Team, Sally Twite, Pam Czerniewska who checked the linguistic details and Julienne Ramsden who selected the texts and also assisted with the collection of data for my research in schools. Recently other members of the OU Research team into textual cohesion have helped me to consolidate some of the ideas presented here, but none of my colleagues are responsible for the flaws the reader will no doubt detect.

Finally, I would like to thank Mrs. Beverley Bell for typing the Manuscript and members of the secretarial staff in the Faculty of Educational Studies for their loyal and invaluable help.

L.John Chapman
1981

The author and publishers wish to thank the following for permission to reproduce copyright material:
Jonathan Cape and the Arthur Ransome Estate for extract from *Swallows and Amazons*; Evans Brothers for extract from *Wurzel Gummidge* by B.E. Todd; Victor Gollancz for extract from *A Wizard of Earthsea* by Ursula Le Guin; Harvard Educational Review for extract from 'The Nature of Literacy' vol 47, August 1977, by Daniel and Lauren Resnick copyright © 1977 by President and Fellows of Harvard College; International Reading Association for extracts from *Journal of Reading* 'An Instructional Application of Cloze

Procedure' (Jan 1973) by R. Bortnick and G. Lopardo and 'On Defining Redundancy in Language' (Jan 1979) by Alice Horning; for extract from *Reading Today International* VIII (4) by Claudia Casey; for extract from *Reading Comprehension at Four Linguistic Levels* introduction by Clifford Pennock (1979); Manchester University Press for extract from 'Reading and Writing' by K. Perara (Chapter 7 of *Language in Infancy and Childhood*: Cruttenden (1979)); *The Times* for extract from 'Languages of the tribe' by Philip Howard 24 Jan 1980; Michael Bond, William Collins (U.K. rights), and Houghton Mifflin (U.S. rights) for extract from *Paddington at Large* (1962); Alan Garner, William Collins (U.K. rights), and Philomel Books (U.S. rights) for extract from *The Weirdstone of Brisingamen* (1960); Gerald Durrell, Granada Publishing (U.K. rights), and Viking Penguin Inc (U.S. rights) for extract from *My Family and Other Animals*.

1 Introduction: decades of change

Changes in school organisation

Since the nineteen sixties there have been considerable changes in
the organisation of schools in Britain. The greatest of these changes
has undoubtedly been the movement towards the comprehen-
sivisation of all state schools. Whilst many have agreed with the
desire for equality of opportunity for all the nation's children – the
ideological driving force behind that movement – the extent to
which these organisational changes must be matched by pedo-
gogical changes has not been appreciated.

In this, the speed with which the organisation of schools can be
changed by administrative procedures can be misleading: the
administrative act is comparatively uncomplicated in itself, whereas
changing the pedagogy of the nation's teaching force is by no means
as straightforward nor can it be so rapid. Combining grammar
school staff who are used to teaching an academic élite with a staff
of a secondary modern school used to catering for the rest of the
population will not overnight bring equality of teaching to all
children. In most areas of the curriculum, and particularly in
literacy and numeracy, the changes require virtual re-training of the
teaching force in both middle and secondary schools.

It is interesting, however, to see how these national and local
changes can be set within a wider movement of educational change
in other western and western type countries. When reading instruction is viewed in an historical perspective, for example, we can see
our problems as part of this wider movement in education. We get a
clear indication of this in the work of Resnick and Resnick (1977)
who examined American and European models of literacy from
such an historical viewpoint and found a 'sharp shift over time in
expectation concerning literacy'. Their survey led them to conclude
that 'reading instruction has been aimed at attaining either a low

level of literacy for a large number of people or a high level for an élite. Thus, the contemporary expectation – high levels of literacy for an entire population – presents a relatively recent development.' And this is surely what is expected of British teachers.

The Resnicks' article makes another point strongly and this should cause us to think further, for they find that the failure of schools to achieve a high level of literacy for all has lent strength to a 'back to the basics' movement in education. They suggest, however, that this is misguided, since their study leads them to the conclusion that 'pedagogical practices from the past offer little remedy for reading problems as currently defined.' They put it thus:

> Although the claim is frequently made that a return to basics would improve our educational systems, the consequences of such a program are not clear. Presumably, proponents of basic education want to stress skills of literacy and mathematics more than certain recent additions to the curriculum. This much is reasonable. But, unless we intend to relinquish the criterion of comprehension as the goal for reading instruction there is little *to go back to* in terms of pedagogical method, curriculum or school organisation. The old tried and true approaches, which nostalgia prompts us to believe might solve current problems, were designed neither to achieve the literacy standard sought today nor to assure successful literacy for everyone. (my italics)

It is clear that we have a formidable problem facing us in the eighties if the goal is the attainment by all of a literary standard previously achieved only by an élite. It is also clear that faced with this challenge retreating to a 'back to basics' methodology is not likely to provide the answers.

The sixties and seventies were characterised not only by these changes but also by increasing amounts of knowledge, particularly of language. This is fortunate for it enables us to propose that to meet the challenge of increasing their pupils' standards of literacy, teachers can draw on the now impressive stock of knowledge of their language and how it works. This will allow them to achieve a higher level of personal knowledge of language upon which to base their classroom teaching. And this strength will provide not only the confidence needed, but the bonus of practical applications for classroom use.

A straightforward relationship is involved. If schools are required to achieve even higher standards of literacy and for all pupils, then the knowledge of their teachers needs to rise commensurately. As Morris (1973) pointed out so succinctly at the ninth annual conference of the United Kingdom Reading Association, 'You can't teach what you don't know.'

Changes in knowledge

Fortunately, as indicated, the sixties and seventies witnessed an upsurge in the amount of research and writing about language. Never before have we had so much knowledge from which to draw insights for our teaching. The science of linguistics and its extension text linguistics, in particular, has enabled us to appreciate new factors about language that were apparently implicit in the language learning situation but about which so little was known to teachers that opportunities to make these factors explicit in classroom situations were not realised. For example, a simple word like *one*, which is taken from the new concept of cohesion, as we shall see later (in Chapter 5), has a number of uses or functions. It can be a simple number, as in '*one*, two, three'; it can act as a pronoun as in, '*one* never knows'; it can mean much the same as 'an'; it can be used as a general noun, but when used as a cohesive substitute for another word that has already been stated is often unnoticed. For example:

I'm disappointed with this new car. The old *one* went much better, this *one* keeps breaking down.

Here *one* stands instead of car on both occasions; it is not a numeral, but a substitute and substitutes help a text 'hang together'. When spelt out like this it seems so obvious. Teachers have been aware of one or two of these functions, but few have realised that 'one' can be a substitute, though this is implicit in our (adult) understanding of a text when reading. But can we assume that our pupils have such understanding? You may appreciate then that when a linguist analyses these different functions effectively, the clarity thus provided gives teachers a firmer knowledge base from which to guide children's language and reading development in the classroom.

One linguist who has stood out in recent decades is Noam Chomsky. His work and that of his followers have given us some basic insights. In his seminal works (Chomsky, 1957 and 1965) on syntax, (the relationship between words in sentences), he provided us with such notions as 'transformational grammar', and 'deep structure', from which the meaning of each sentence is derived. His work also revived debates as to the origins of human language – whether it is innate or learned. His ideas acted as a catalyst to research work and an upsurge of research papers (see Smith and Wilson, 1979) on language followed his publications. However, whilst we acknowledge the important effects his work had, this book does not use his insights, as they were restricted to the sentence. For reading development a global perspective is needed to take us beyond the boundary of the sentence.

Other linguists, notably those concerned with anthropological studies, have been attempting to record the previously unrecorded (spoken) languages of people living in remote places and to explore the intricacies of their various tongues. In their work they have had to look to longer stretches of language than the sentence and to examine the resources these languages have for connecting them. Some, for example Sinclair and Coulthard (1975), have demonstrated how smaller units like sentences and paragraphs are combined into overall discourse. Much has been learned from these and other studies, such as the way in which we know how the topic of the conversation is highlighted and how and when people take turns in being the speaker as they interact with each other in conversation.

During the past two decades, we have seen how traditional linguistic notions have broadened and now employ other areas of study. This interdisciplinary development, which is now known as text linguistics has great potential for helping teachers to appreciate what is entailed in the reading process.

Of all the topics that have contributed to text linguistics and that might supply insights to the study of reading 'artificial intelligence' appears, at first, the most unlikely. However, to get a machine to 'understand' involves making explicit those features of language that, because of their implicitness, have been taken for granted and, therefore, not explored by teachers in their teaching.

The following example from artificial intelligence gives some idea of these factors. Until a computer's store of world knowledge holds as much as is stored in the human memory, the machine is unlikely to be able to understand natural language as a human being can. In Chapter 9 there is an example of the extent of knowledge we have of one ordinary everyday vocabulary item, a piggy-bank. Just glance at pages 119 to 20 to see the extent of this information. To make sense of its use requires a store of facts that might be taken for granted in teaching situations until written down like this and their extent displayed for us. These facts are greatly in excess of what an ordinary dictionary would supply. We assume all too readily in our language behaviour that children have the same amount of detailed commonsense knowledge of the world as we have, when all too often they only have that knowledge partially. And yet fullness of knowledge is crucial to the comprehending process.

This is most important during reading instruction. An individual child may well recognise a word and be able to say it aloud, but we cannot know from this how complete the concept is that lies behind the sound. For comprehending, the child often requires different facets of that concept in order to understand fully the passage being read. The danger inherent in gauging reading progress by, for example, graded word reading tests, becomes obvious from this one insight from artificial intelligence.

Other areas of language study provide us with more assistance. In addition to Chomsky's explanations of syntax that we have mentioned above, semantics, the study of meaning, has also made great advances. And more recently pragmatics, which points out the importance of the intention that lies behind the actual words we use, is another area of growing interest (Bates, 1976). For example, we often say something like;

'Your coat's on the floor.'

Our intention is more than a statement as to the position of a coat. The pragmatic force behind the words produces a meaning more like:

'Your coat's on the floor, pick it up at once, and hang it where it should be.'

These are but one or two examples of the insights that are becoming available to teachers.

In the eighties we may be faced with ever-increasing demands, but at least we have a store of new knowledge that is either directly applicable to the solution of classroom problems or gives us clearer insights that help us to understand how problems might arise. Armed with such a knowledge base we ought to be able to prevent them arising in the first place. This requires a process of continual up-dating by means of personal reading and adequate in-service education.

Changes in teacher education

Along with the increasing demands made upon the education system and the changes in its organisation have come changes in teacher education. The sixties and seventies saw an enormous expansion in teacher education with colleges adopting an industrial style shift system, and higher levels of qualification such as the introduction of the B.Ed. and the announcement of an all-graduate entry to the profession in the early eighties. And yet, owing to the fall in the birthrate, the seventies ended with contraction. Further reorganisation of the structure of colleges of education and their diversification began and will continue into the eighties.

Some of the problems that have arisen out of a combination of these movements and society's demands for increasing skills in literacy are still far from being solved. It is still not clear whether or not our present programmes for the initial training of teachers are preparing teachers sufficiently well to enter schools to begin their work of teaching the children of the eighties.

While many laudable features have been introduced into B.Ed. courses and have demonstrably improved the quality of teaching, the demands that society is making of the schools are still not reflected in these new training programmes. All too often the newly trained enter the profession with an inadequate knowledge base of language and how it functions. Attempts have been made to improve matters (see CNAA 'Guidelines for Language and Literacy' in B.Ed. proposals) but there is still much to be done.

In-service education, especially the type that focuses on the school's interpretation of its own needs, requires further development and resources and a higher level of basic training and staff development.

Broadening the concept of reading

In this book I am suggesting that the concept of reading has, over the past decade, expanded considerably. If, for example, you ask the man or woman in the street or even a teacher in a middle or secondary school, what he or she understands by teaching children to read, then the answer is often in terms of 'teaching them to sound their letters'. It is as though the phonic method of teaching reading, in the stage sometimes called 'code-cracking', is what reading is all about. After this has been achieved it is as though the child is thought to be able to read from then on throughout life without further teaching support.

Teachers are beginning to realise that reading, while admittedly having an important decoding process built into it, is a vastly more complicated affair, mastery of which extends well beyond the infant school into the years of secondary schooling and, indeed, beyond.

In an introduction to a book he edited for the International Reading Association, Pennock (1979) puts the problem like this:

> Beyond the first years of school, reading growth of children seems to drop. Possibly this results from continuing emphasis (whether needed or not) on language units smaller than the word, thereby short-changing children's needs in learning to comprehend the word, sentence, paragraph, and beyond or, as Shuy suggests, discourse in processing of meaning units.
>
> In many cases, however, superfluous decoding instruction would not seem to be the cause of decreased reading growth as children move beyond the primary grades. In many cases, decoding instruction is discontinued as children master decoding. Unfortunately, the position is sometimes taken that little further systematic reading instruction is necessary on the wishful assumption that decoding proficiency equals reading with meaning.

The history of reading instruction and reading research has not encouraged this development and the move to consider reading as being concerned with longer stretches of text may be slow to come. The decades preceding the seventies saw many debates centred around what method should be used to teach children how to recover the language locked up, as it were, in the black squiggles on the page. These debates have occupied teachers and researchers for many years and it is ironic that it now appears that it does not matter very much which method is used for the formal instruction of the skill as most children will learn to read irrespective of method.

The Danish writers, Jansen et al. (1978), in a delightful book entitled *The Teaching of Reading Without Really Any Method*, are seemingly almost oblivious to problems that have beset American and British teachers for years. We suspect, however, that they are just commenting in a friendly way on our preoccupation with the phonic/whole-word debate.

As with the debates of teachers on methodology so it has been with much of the reading research effort. Here too we have witnessed a concentration on smaller and smaller elements, the minutiae of reading which are involved in these beginning stages. It would seem, as I have pointed out elsewhere (Chapman, 1979a), that a mode of reading research has been taken from the physical sciences where researchers have pursued smaller and smaller particles. In reading, researchers have investigated the smallest features of perception, not just words and letters but those very small parts of letters that distinguish one letter from another when flashed on a screen by a tachistoscope for a split second.

Now this is not to deny the very valuable facts that have emerged and are still emerging from research into perceptual processes using such technical apparatus as tachistoscopes in laboratories. The recent work of Tony Marcel (1978) into unconscious perceptual processing clearly demonstrates the value of these efforts. However, there can be little doubt that, for the educationalist, the importance of reading lies in the acquisition of knowledge from large chunks of text. The important thing for the teacher, therefore, is to discover how children come to be able to put these larger units of texts together, to reassemble, if you like, the author's message. This is the view adopted here: it does not matter what the reading purpose is as long as it exists. Your interest may lie in reading to gain specific information for everyday living, or it may be for a very specialist subject, or again in a study of literature. In the main, on most occasions in schools, children are involved in reading larger units of continuous texts rather than single sentences.

It follows, therefore, that in order to meet the aims of the school curriculum as far as reading is concerned, an interest in the way in which texts are organised will prove most useful. Furthermore, if we can specify which parts of the text help us to recognise how the text is put together, it will assist us to reassemble or recreate its meaning for ourselves during reading.

From this you will gather that the smallest unit of reading that we shall focus on will be the word or groups of words but then only to learn how such words or groups of words link longer elements such as sentences together to create textual cohesion.

Reading viewed in this way applies not only to the infant and junior school, but as much, or even more to the middle and secondary school. This is not to say that the teachers of younger children will not find this book useful, for some of the most important words from the point of view of cohesion are also some of the first to be taught. They are those small, frequently used words that so often occur on flashcards and in graded word reading texts. Here, although we are interested in their instant recognition, it is the job they do in the text, or as we would prefer to say their function or functions, that will concern us most.

Summary

We have seen in this first chapter something of the changes that have been taking place in schools and the demands these changes and society's expectations make upon them. Alongside this we noted that there has been a considerable increase in the knowledge we have of language and how it works in communication. This new text linguistic knowledge provides teachers with many implements with which to carry out some of their tasks so as to improve their effectiveness in classrooms. We saw also that our concept of reading has expanded to include a broader framework of skills than the initial decoding operations. Such a concept is required to cope with the many purposes to which reading is put in the school curriculum for these involve comprehending long stretches of text.

2 Reading: an expanding concept

Comprehension

For the purpose of talking about standards, it is helpful to look at the 'end-product' of the teaching of reading. This is usually thought to be comprehension because comprehension is often regarded as being measurable and thereby assessable. You will have noticed perhaps in the quotation from Resnick and Resnick on page 2 the clause, 'unless we relinquish the criterion of comprehension'. Obviously standards are related to comprehension or pupils' understanding of what is read. However, what many teachers mean by understanding what is read is really 'learning' from what is read. When reading is required of pupils, for example from a textbook, it really means 'learn the subject content in the text'.

To raise standards, or to achieve the standards expected, we clearly need to find out a lot more of what goes on during the process of comprehending, and to view comprehending as an active learning process. You will find, therefore, in the chapters that follow that the focus is on the act of comprehending rather than on the end product, comprehension. You may have had an indication of this already from the list of this book's contents, where the word 'comprehending' rather than 'comprehension' is chosen deliberately for the title of the final chapter. Chapter 9 attempts to integrate the eight earlier chapters by summarising them in terms of comprehending.

Assisting comprehending

To understand more of the act of comprehending we need to look at many factors that affect how we read and what happens when we read. Teachers need to be concerned with these insights for they will shed light on those aspects of reading that respond to direct teaching or instruction. Furthermore, they will indicate where a teacher might intervene most profitably to assist the growth of the skill of comprehending. One basic method for doing this is outlined in Chapter 8.

Curriculum demands on reading

As we have seen, the need to look again seriously at the way we organise and teach reading arises from society's desire to make all its children literate. But it is more than this, society also requires schools to prepare its children for its own complexity. Without these twin, in some ways interrelated demands, children would not have to submit themselves to the rigours of learning to read and write to ever increasing levels of competence. The high levels of literacy for the entire population as described by Resnick and Resnick are necessary for children to be able to cope with modern living and its reflection in the school curriculum.

The danger for schools is that if further additions are made to the curriculum the time that is necessary to teach children to read to the standards required may be reduced. And yet reading may be the skill mostly employed for learning the content of subjects in the curriculum, including so many of the recent additions.

The effects of these demands are exacerbated by our present school organisation and practices so that children are seen not to be coping with their reading. An illustration of this can be found in the report of the Schools Council Project, *The Effective Use of Reading* (Lunzer and Gardner, 1979) where details of what happens to progress in reading in the first year of secondary school are given:

> For average and above average pupils, the experience of meaningful reading across the curriculum becomes stabilised, or even regresses at first year levels, and has low priority throughout the pre-examination years . . . A fundamental necessity is to provide the pupils with a meaningful experience of reading in science, social studies, mathematics and English. (p.135)

From the Project's classroom observation data we find differences in the pattern of lessons between top-junior and first-year secondary classes. These differences were signalled by:

1 a decrease in individual tuition and an increase in 'teacher informing' at first year secondary level;

2 a significant increase in pupil time spent 'listening' at first year secondary level;

3   a marked increase in the use of textbooks in all subjects except mathematics at first-year level.

Furthermore the Project points to another complicating factor regarding the texts themselves. Harrison puts it thus:

> What we would suggest is that the results of our research, taken together with parallel findings from similar studies, give firm evidence that many students, perhaps even most students, learn less than they might otherwise do from school texts, and this is because texts are presenting difficulties not just in terms of conceptual context, but because of ways in which they are written. (p.101)

It would appear from this research that children are not prepared for the changes in the curriculum demands of secondary schools, and that the texts that are provided for them to read are themselves adding to their reading problems. It would seem that the schools have not yet evolved the necessary organisation and teaching strategies to meet the demands. This is understandable as it is only during the last few years that the true position has been identified and the textual problem recognised. The developmental perspective that now engages our thinking is along the 'learning to read: reading to learn' continuum (Chapman, 1980a). As we may now begin to appreciate, the great problem is the narrowness of our concept of reading in education.

A restricted concept of reading

To achieve reading standards at the level that society is beginning to require, teachers will need to move from the position of 'decoding proficiency equals reading with meaning' to one which encompasses a much wider language comprehending approach. And, as mentioned earlier, this will need considerable in-service education and private reading by teachers to move to a position where the broader concept works through into classroom practice.

A wider concept of reading

Many writers over the years have viewed reading as an activity that involves the higher thought processes, and statements of this relationship continue to appear. For example it has been associated with 'reasoning' again recently by Downing (1979) in his book *Reading and Reasoning*. Defined in this way reading must involve much more of our pupils' growing cognitive ability than is required by the initial stage of deciphering the print although this retains its importance in the early stages. Reading is, after all, a manifestation of our ability to communicate through language. As such it will involve the fundamental relationship between language and thought which was put so well by Vygotsky (1962): 'Thought is not merely expressed in words; it comes into existence through them.' Developing reading, therefore, must be seen within a much wider concept, for only in this way will it get the teaching support throughout schooling that it needs to achieve curriculum aims.

Reading can be seen as a confirmation of language acquisition. As such it has its roots, as Halliday has shown, in the child's desire to influence and make sense of his environment: he 'learns how to mean' (Halliday, 1975, p.58). This view and many other findings from language research generally are applicable to reading, and the most significant ones are outlined in Chapter 3.

Reading as communication

In order to spell out further the place of reading in a wider language context we borrow some concepts from communication engineers. It is salutary to remind ourselves of this, for reading is a form of communication through language.

At its simplest the bases of human communication are a message originator, the thoughts, ideas or information that he or she intends to convey and another person to receive them. The contents of the communication – the thoughts, ideas or information – are usually encoded into some form of language which shapes them and, as we are unlikely to master the art of direct thought transference in the forseeable future, that language is transmitted by the sound waves of speech to the listener or hearer.

Assuming that both the sender and receiver of the message are of the same language community, are fluent in that language and have no physical or other handicaps, the hearer receives the sounds, retrieves (decodes) the language and is thence able to share, to a greater or lesser extent, the ideas or thoughts of the originator of the message. This appears to be a fairly straightforward and remarkably efficient process. And indeed it is, provided that when the language form is speech three important conditions exist. These are that both the speaker and hearer are in the same place at the same time and share the same language.

The implicit context of speech

Notice first the importance of time and place, for, in some ways, writing was born of the necessity to overcome their restrictions. If the speaker, for example, speaks to me today and I am not with him till tomorrow, then no communication will have taken place. Similarly, if the speaker addresses a message to me, and, at that very moment I am in another place out of earshot it does not matter how intently I am listening or how loudly the speaker shouts, the communication process will have been abortive. When messages are conveyed by normal speech the physical situation is the context.

Technology and communication

Some of the environmental features associated with speech have been blurred by modern technology which has made considerable progress in overcoming some of the drawbacks of the short-ranged transitory nature of speech by transmitting sound over distance by telephone or radio. We can also make and send sound recordings on magnetic tapes or disks round the world and beyond. These are modern attempts to release us from the confines of the here and now, by making the transitory nature of speech more permanent. Paradoxically, these technological advances sometimes suffer from

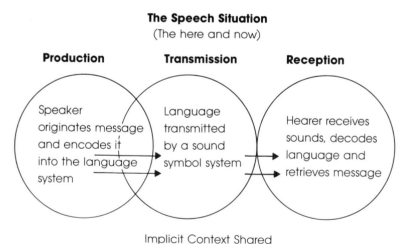

The Speech Situation
(The here and now)

| **Production** | **Transmission** | **Reception** |

Speaker originates message and encodes it into the language system

Language transmitted by a sound symbol system

Hearer receives sounds, decodes language and retrieves message

Implicit Context Shared

Figure 1. The implicit context of speech

some of the same and other restrictions which arise out of the very technology being employed. The radio message, for instance, is usually broadcast at a set time and may be missed or suffer atmospheric interference (static); tape and disk recordings need play-back facilities and power to operate them, conditions which are not always readily available when needed or suffer deterioration, as does the power source of a dying satellite.

The telephone comes near to releasing us from the 'here' of 'here and now' and its ubiquity pays tribute to its effectiveness. However, the time dimension still applies for we have to be present to receive the message in order to respond to the sender of the message as in conversation.

The explicit context of print

When sound is used to transmit the message, time and location are seen to be crucial. This is important not only from the point-of-view of the transitory nature of sound waves in that we might not be able to hear for purely physical reasons, but in another important respect, which is that some of the meaning of the message resides in the immediate situation in which the communication takes place. Indeed, as Stenning (1978) points out, 'Not only are people and

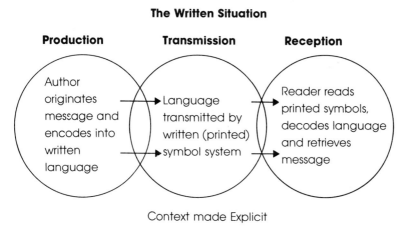

Context made Explicit

Figure 2. The explicit context of print

things obvious in the speech situation, the speaker and hearer usually share the scenario that provides *continuity*.' (my italics)

Now, when the message sender is an author, that is, he is encoding his message directly into written language, we must note that as he constructs his text he takes for granted that his readers have at least two types of knowledge on which to draw in order to understand his message fully. These are firstly, prior knowledge of the world (prior knowledge in the sense that the knowledge is present before the text is read), and, secondly, knowledge of the language system. We take these two types of knowledge for granted in the speech situation, but in texts some of the implicit situation of speech has to be made explicit.

Prior knowledge

The first type of knowledge that we take for granted in writing is the level of knowledge of the reader. This awareness of audience is important. As I write now, for example, I assume that my readers will be mostly teachers and from contact with many such teachers I know roughly the base level of prior knowledge that I can build upon, or at least I think I do! If you find comprehending hard going as you read this, I may have taken too much for granted. Every teacher will know the adage 'start your teaching from where the child is' and we certainly do this in conversation, receiving all kinds of feedback of a verbal and non-verbal nature to assure us that our message has been received and understood. When we are writing we assume a prior knowledge base but we are without that feedback of the speech situation.

This extra-linguistic knowledge, facets of which we will discuss again later, is used a great deal in comprehending a passage. Some of you may have come across the work of Tuinman (1974) who in his discussion of comprehension showed that some readers could answer many of the questions they were to be asked before they read the passage. They answered in the main from their prior knowledge of the world. That we are to supply this knowledge is signalled in a variety of ways; in speech by reference to features in the immediate situation but outside the actual words of the conversation (to 'the here and now' of the situation), and in writing by the same knowledge of how language functions in the speech situation and by explicit cues and descriptions supplied by the author.

Prior knowledge: literacy specific

We should not underestimate the importance of this prior knowledge, for we engage some of it even before we open a book to begin to read. A skilled reader will be aware when selecting a book from the library shelves or buying it from a bookshop, that it is fiction or non-fiction. His prior knowledge of different types of text guides him in this. If, for example, he chooses Salinger (1958) *The Catcher in the Rye*, no matter what his purpose was in its selection his anticipation of what is to be read is causing predictions to occur before he even reads the first page. He may already know something of the author, what style he employs and so on. In other words he begins to set the scene for reading by alerting his memory schemata (see Chapter 9) in various ways. Schemata are collections of related facts about the world, in this case, about reading certain authors, texts and so on, which have been built up over a long period and stored in memory. These are constantly being addressed, up-dated and amended. Thus our reader has already anticipated the type of text and is prepared for certain formats to occur – he will expect the author to introduce his main characters and the situation – and so it is, for he has selected from his memory schemata this type of fictional style and all that that involves, or else, if he has not met him in print before, he is ready to search his schemata of 'fiction' to add to or contrast this latest example. (Adams and Collins (1979) give a useful description of schema-theoretic models of language comprehension.)

Prior knowledge and knowledge frames

As the actual text is being read, further schemata are alerted and are soon brought into play. In the Salinger novel referred to above for example, the author relies a great deal on his reader's prior knowledge of literature as well as the world in which we live.

It has been proposed recently (e.g. Minsky, 1975; Fillmore, 1976) that some of this world knowledge can be thought of as being organised within 'frames'. A frame might be alerted for example by the word 'restaurant' in a text. From this word and from the context being created by the author, we anticipate restaurant-type behaviour and words associated with restaurants. The reader alerted to such a 'frame' will not be surprised if the description in the text involves sitting at a table and expecting to be served with food and drink. It is suggested that such a frame would encompass the whole notion of paying someone to prepare and provide food, and the whole visit to a restaurant would be conducted as a pleasant activity. Such frames are described as prototypes: that is, in this example, not one particular restaurant but of restaurants in general. Fillmore (op. cit.) puts forward his proposal thus:

> First, the meanings of words may, more than we are used to thinking, depend on contexted experiences. . . . Second, the process of interpreting an utterance may depend, more than we are used to thinking, on our perception of the context in which the utterance is produced and our memories of the contexts for earlier experiences with the utterance or its constituent parts.

This is a powerful insight for teachers of reading, no matter which age-group is being taught, for if you include these notions within an extended concept of reading that views reading as active text reconstruction, then possibilities for application soon spring to mind. The teacher could, for example, as a preparation for reading a particular text, discuss some of the key concepts to be met by relating them directly to the experiences of the children. Words that might prove difficult could also be discussed in such a way as to relate them both to the content of the text and to the existing knowledge of the children.

Knowledge frames and fluent reading

We often talk of skilled reading as being fluent, and there can be little doubt that much of that fluency depends on the ability to anticipate what is to come in the text. It can be seen from the discussion above that when readers appreciate the frame or frames within which the author is working, they are better able to predict what is to come semantically or, to put it in simpler terms, from the overall meaning of that part of the passage. Having recognised this, the teacher's job becomes a little clearer, for if, as is suggested, frames accrue from experience and this includes experience through reading, then activities that help to build up and organise those experiences should assist the comprehending process. Where necessary, that is where there are indications that frames have not been built up or where they are incomplete, then to work on this in various ways on topics to be read about *before* reading, will assist later reading fluency and, thereby, comprehending.

Summarising so far, we might say that the concept of reading that is being related views reading as a language activity through which the reader re-creates the author's message using a variety of cues in the text (Ryan and Semmel, 1969). This direct use of the text is supplemented by prior literary knowledge of texts, authors and the language of books, as well as knowledge of the world and of specific subject topics. The reader forms hypotheses about what the author intended to mean and these are confirmed or otherwise as reading proceeds. We are now a long way from the concept of reading as simply that of the initial stages. It is a process that uses many facets of human ability, especially our knowledge of language. We go on next, therefore, to look further at language and how linguists describe it.

Linguistic knowledge
Many of the points raised above can be subsumed under our knowledge of language, but for educational purposes and for the instructional improvements desired, we need a more detailed description of more specific areas of language. Some linguists are beginning to provide that type of knowledge.

Linguistics, and more recently text linguistics, is a highly specialised field of study with its own technical vocabulary. It is also a field of study which has not been without controversy for many of the relatively few years it has existed. For this reason we should not be surprised if linguists disagree, for they often do. At least it points to their studies being alive and vigorous.

There is often confusion about the word 'linguist' to start with, for the generally accepted notion of a linguist is of someone who can speak a number of languages. This, however, is not necessarily what we understand to be the job of linguists who work in university departments of linguistics. They may or may not be fluent in many languages; rather their concern is to analyse and explain how language works. They have a certain perspective on language which is based, according to Gordon (1979), on a framework of basic assumptions. Some of these are referred to in the next chapter so here we will only clear the ground a little by pointing to some potential confusions.

Aitchison (1978) whose outline we follow, suggests that linguistics is often confused by some teachers with the old style of 'school' grammar that was the base of many children's language work before and in many cases since, the war. One thing is quite clear, modern linguistics is significantly different from traditional grammar. First of all, it is descriptive rather than prescriptive. It reports and analyses what is said or written, not what ought to be said or written. Linguistics, then, does not involve itself with 'correctness'.

A second important characteristic of linguistics is the emphasis that is given to the spoken rather than the written word. This emphasis has been increased by the use of electronic recording which has caught and held 'utterances' so as to allow detailed analysis.

The third difference that distinguishes linguistics from the earlier type of school grammar is the abandonment of the Latin-based framework. As Aitchison (op.cit.) puts it:

> Linguists are opposed to the notion that any one language can provide an adequate framework for all the others. They are trying to set up a universal framework. And there is no reason why this should resemble the grammar of Latin, or the grammar of any other language arbitrarily selected from the many thousands spoken by mankind.

These are three important characteristics of linguistics to which a fourth needs adding. This is that the descriptions of language should be rigorous. Linguistics can be regarded then as the systematic study of language.

Aitchison (op.cit.) gives a 'rough impression of the range of topics covered' by modern linguistics in a diagram which we have modified as Figure 3.

The area of knowledge covered, as the diagram indicates, is vast and continues to expand rapidly. Because of this and the introductory nature of this book I have had to be very selective. The selection has been achieved by constantly bearing in mind two related guidelines:

1   which parts of this linguistic knowledge will provide insights to teachers for a better understanding of language and how it develops;

2   which part of its technical array, suitably modified, might be used directly in classrooms.

You will see in the Aitchison diagram that there are four main circles radiating outwards. In the centre is phonetics, the study of human speech sounds, and while this is an essential study for the student of linguistics, it is more by way of background for most primary and secondary teachers. However, for the teacher of young children, both phonetics and phonology should be of considerable importance (see Czerniewska *et al.* (1979) for an introduction for teachers). Phonetics is surrounded by phonology (sound patterning) in the

Figure 3.   Topics covered by linguistics and their relationship to other disciplines. From Aitchison (1978 p.16).

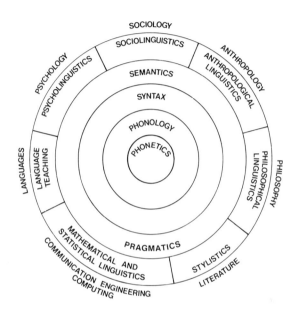

diagram and phonetics and phonology are surrounded by syntax which refers 'to both the arrangement and the form of words. Semantics (meaning) is placed in the circle outside syntax, and next to the various disciplines which link linguistics with the external world.' In many accounts, the three areas, phonology, syntax and semantics are covered by the more general term grammar. We add pragmatics to the circle which is labelled semantics as this is a growing addition to our understanding of language.

Grammar
There is more than one account of grammar that could be looked at, for example *The Grammar of Contemporary English* by Quirk *et al.* (1972) or Chomsky's (1957, 1965) *Transformational Grammar*. However, the work selected is that of Michael Halliday and the systemic grammarians. (see Kress (1976), Halliday (1978b), Berry (1975, 1977)). This has been chosen as it appears to have been inspired by features that find responses amongst school teachers.

These same features are shown by Halliday to be significant in early language situations as the child learns how to mean (Halliday, 1975).

Halliday's notions of grammar are based on the fundamental importance of the functions of language to express the world around us and inside us. Language is an act. As such it functions in three basic ways which are:

1   an interpersonal function – that is, to maintain and specify relations between members of societies;

2   an ideational function – to transmit information between members of society;

3   a textual function – the organisation of discourse as relevant to the situation.

Halliday (1975) suggests that the first two functions, interpersonal and ideational, are not separate in the early stages of language development. So, for example, a child's utterance, 'more meat', was always combined with what is called a pragmatic function, that is, with a meaning that has a command built into it i.e. 'I want more meat'. As the child matures the two become separated and later it becomes possible for the child to, as it were, step outside language to investigate it.

Sentence functions are, therefore, ideational and interpersonal. The ideational component of language is largely conveyed by the internal grammatical structure of the sentence (the relationships between noun and verbs etc.) and the interpersonal by sentence type (e.g. command, question or statement).

The functional approach, as Fletcher (1979) says, 'with its emphasis on language behaviour and language use, is of considerable interest to anyone concerned with language learning in the child, and can be followed up on a number of publications by Halliday and his associates'. For an introduction to this work and to systemic grammar which evolved from Halliday's work, see Berry (1975, 1977), Fletcher (1979).

Summary
In this chapter we have noted the importance of reading in the modern curriculum and the dangers that are attendant on it if it does not receive teaching support throughout the years of compulsory schooling.

In this we have outlined a concept of reading as communication, which is then greatly expanded from the popular concept of reading that applies to 'code-cracking' in the beginning stages. This wider concept is based on a continuation of language development along the continuum 'learning to read: reading to learn', and as such involves new insights coming from the study of language. These insights distinguish firstly between spoken and written language. However, we note that a knowledge of these features of spoken language are assumed by the author who helps the reader build up the situational context that would have pertained in that speech situation. Decoding the print to speech is only a part of the process. What has to be alerted is the knowledge of how language functions in continuous texts, that is text linguistics.

The importance of the level of prior knowledge assumed by the author was outlined as consisting of two types, prior knowledge of the world and prior knowledge of language. The former was subdivided for teaching purposes into specific literacy knowledge and common (or world) knowledge. It was suggested that this knowledge was stored in memory schemata in knowledge frames.

While discussing prior knowledge of language, the importance of the fairly new branch of study, linguistics, was emphasised by showing how its assumptions differ from those of old-style school grammar. The work of Halliday, his functional (systemic) grammar, was proposed as being more appropriate to teaching than most others.

3 Language development and reading

As we noted in the previous chapter, the study of language falls into three main areas: syntactics, the relationship between words in sentences; semantics, the relationship between words and their references; and pragmatics, the relationship between words and the way they are used. You may remember that pragmatics was added to syntactics and semantics at the centre of the diagram on page 21. This is because pragmatics is a fairly recent study whose importance is only just beginning to make its appearance in the literature (Lock, 1980). I mention its effects from time to time but do not deal with it in this section on language development. For those who wish to study how children acquire pragmatics a book by Bates (1976) is worth consulting.

Language acquisition

One area of increasing knowledge has come from studies in language acquisition, where the child's first language has been charted in some detail (see Brown, 1973, for a masterly study). Unfortunately, language development after initial phases, that is, during the years of compulsory schooling, is not so well documented. What is more, some of the pronouncements of the early psycholinguists about the rapidity of language acquisition could have been misleading when viewed from an educational perspective. The following statement of David McNeill (1966), for instance, is still often quoted:

> At the age of about one, a normal child, not impaired by hearing loss or speech impediment, will begin to say words. By one-and-a-half or two years, he will begin to form simple two and three word sentences. By four years, he will have mastered very nearly the complex and abstract

structure of the English language. In slightly more than two years, therefore, children acquire full knowledge of the grammatical system of their native tongue.

Some teachers might be forgiven if they gained the impression from such enthusiastic statements that there would be little by way of language development for them to promote if children, by four years of age, have 'acquired full knowledge of the grammatical system'. But this would conflict with the evidence before them in school. Most teachers are only too well aware that a great deal of language development needs to take place during the years of compulsory schooling. How then can such psycholinguistic statements be reconciled with the day-to-day experiences of the practising teachers? The psycholinguists were highlighting the speed with which the normal child masters speech. However, as Fagan (1971/72) pointed out:

> Although children may be fluent in their use of oral language and may have acquired control over the basic sentence patterns of the English language by the time they enter school, it does not follow that this fluency will automatically transfer to written language structures. Furthermore, although a child may have acquired the basic patterns of the language by the time he enters school, it must be remembered that the task of manipulating more and more complex structures still lies before him.

The initial acquisition phase is very rapid indeed and those who study the complexity of the task continue to express wonderment. What has to take place by way of future language development is just as remarkable. The child, having acquired his first language and internalised it without, as it were, realising it, *now has to become conscious of it* in order to continue to master the skills of literacy. This process is at the heart of language development and becomes more noticeable as the child learns to read and write.

It is important to emphasise that few developmental studies have been carried out to give us detailed guidance as to what features of language are developing during the years of schooling, their rates of development, and what kinds of teaching strategies are needed to encourage progress. We should also note that much of the early acquisition research that has been documented was in terms of the sentence, and how children learn to order their newly learned words into syntactic patterns. Although syntax is very important, children are simultaneously acquiring other systems of the language process such as the semantic (meaning) and pragmatic (intention) systems, which depend a great deal on maturation and experience. When these other systems are related to the socialisation process also taking place, we do not need much imagination to realise that children at school will need all the support their teachers can give to assist their language development.

While we await the research necessary to help with such tasks as monitoring pupils' language progress in schools (Bullock, 1975) we can study the findings of scholars, linguists, psycholinguists, sociologists, those who study artificial intelligence, text linguists and indeed other teachers. In this way we can make some informed guesses to help guide classroom work, rather than being led by what is often called, pejoratively, 'the language folklore of teachers'.

The implicit features of language

A common remark of teachers is that some children take to school language tasks 'like ducks to water'. By this they usually mean that one or two children will acquire reading and writing skills with very little difficulty, almost without any formal instruction (see Clark, 1977). It is as though some children are, to use a computer analogy, pre-programmed to pick up reading in much the same way as Chomsky (1965) proposes that children are pre-programmed to acquire their first language. On the other hand, there are many who do not display such language facility in the classroom, and who need a great deal of teaching and understanding. It is likely that the linguistic features of interest are those that we take for granted. They are learned or picked up by some, implicitly. As Halliday (1978) has put it: 'to know a language means to control its resources at a level below that of conscious awareness'. If we examine some of these facets more closely we may be able to begin to account for some of the apparent discrepancies in language abilities. Having done so, we might also be better able to help those who experience difficulty acquiring literacy.

Language variation

One of the characteristics of language that has achieved some prominence in discussion amongst linguists for some time is language variation. Crystal (1975) has also pointed out its neglect in the study of reading. Fortunately, these insights are now beginning to percolate through to the educational world. For a useful intro-

duction see O'Donnell and Todd (1980) and O.U. Course PE232
Language Development (1979), for teaching implications.

Dialect

In a sense, teachers have always been aware of the rich variety of
language that surrounds them, but have not carried the interpretation
of the finer detail of these varieties and their implications through to
the classroom situation. There are many widely differing varieties
of English in use in this country, and in other English-speaking
countries abroad, like the Caribbean and North America, and it is
surprising, perhaps, how easily a native speaker of English can
understand them.

Look at these pertinent comments by Philip Howard (1980) in
his review of the new book by Michaels and Ricks (1979).

> The notion of correct (or Queen's, or standard) English has become a
> difficult one for our generation which is correctly suspicious of
> authority. Like what we bees needin is beaucoup cognizance that
> brothers and sisters rappin on am not necessarily talkin a substandard
> creole, but don disprove that in living vibrant color. That may be
> incorrect *Times* style, liable to make the sub-editor purse his lips and
> the night lawyer wake up with a start. But it is correct in Watts County,
> where the language of *The Times* would seem, if spoken, grotesquely
> stuffy, alien, and unintelligible. Each of us uses many different
> dialects (in this book we distinguish the term dialect from register) of
> English, for different occasions (writing to one's bank manager,
> writing an informal letter, talking to a friend, talking to a stranger,
> talking on the dreadful telephone . . .) and each dialect is 'correct' in its
> proper context. What goes wrong is not deviation from some rational
> absolute standard of correctitude, but the use of an inappropriate
> dialect in an incongrous context, as in, 'Ta-ta. Your Holiness, baby; see
> you soon, luv'.

This group of regional varieties is often referred to as dialect. Brook
(1973) defines dialect as 'a sub-division of a language that is used by
a group of speakers who have some non-linguistic characteristic in
common.' In most cases this is a particular geographical area. It is
true that some dialects diverge from the standard dialect so much
that it is sometimes difficult for those of one dialect to understand a
speaker of another, but on the whole an adult native speaker of
English can usually understand most dialects of English. You could
probably make sense of the illustration given above. But how do we
help children to cope with this wealth of variety?

On the one hand we would wish to encourage the rich force-fulness of a local dialect and yet, on the other hand, we know that the standard dialect is necessary to give children some semblance of equality for job opportunity in the present social setting. The dilemma for teachers was shown in a recent publication where Charles Mungo (1979), Deputy Head of Upton House School, Hackney, was unequivocal about giving all our pupils some competence in the standard dialect. He says that the most useful dialect we know is standard English or 'Internationally Accepted English', as he calls it. Mr Mungo has no hesitation in saying that the educator's task is to take the dialect speaker as far as possible along the language continuum towards standard English. One of the basic assumptions made clear by linguists (Gordon, 1979) is that no one variety of the language is linguistically better for communication, or of greater worth than another. All appear to convey meaning effectively. However, to be strictly accurate, perhaps we ought to say that, as yet, linguists have no effective way of measuring the linguistic superiority, if any, of one variation over another. The apparent superiority of standard English comes from the prestige of those who speak it, and not from any inherent linguistic quality. Viv Richards (1979) on the other hand, writing in the same journal as Charles Mungo, points out that the school must also accept the dialect speaker, for the insistence on standard English, no matter how sympathetically presented, is likely to be perceived by children as a variation on the theme: 'Your language is wrong: ours is right'. Nevertheless, the language expected by many employers is the variety spoken in the South of England, exemplified by the dialect and accent of the BBC news presenter.

Register

As well as regional variation or dialect, you will find that the same person will switch from one variety to another, as we saw in the quote from Howard above, according to the social or occupational situation in which he finds himself. The same man will use one variety when speaking to his wife and children, another when addressing a public meeting, and still another when in his club or the local pub. The term often used for variation according to situation is 'register'. It has been suggested that the special language used by teachers when teaching their subjects, the language of mathematics, of science and other technical subjects, for instance, is a type of register (for a useful introduction, see the Australian *Journal of Reading*, Vol. 2. (4) (1979). This instructional register, as it has been called, often presents learners with problems, since so much prior knowledge tends to be taken for granted. As Downing (1976) has shown, teachers of reading use a reading instruction register which has its own vocabulary. Teachers use words like 'letter', 'sound', 'beginning', 'middle', 'end', 'word', 'sentence' in their teaching, assuming that children understand, but unfortunately many do not. Later in secondary school, indeed throughout schooling, the same process can be seen at work. Johns (1979) presents some interesting work in this area including some activities to promote language skills in general.

Some of the register variations are more subtle than those exemplified by dialects. The variety of language used by the child in the home for instance, will have its own characteristics and regularities and will be a quite adequate means of expression within the intimacy of the family. The child will be able to convey his meaning in order to have his needs satisfied. There will be an informality about the home variety but its appropriateness is restricted to the confines of the individual family. However acceptable the home variety may be, it will be detrimental to the growing child in his adaptation to the world outside the home if he or she does not have experience of other varieties.

The variety of language met in the school is again different, having other preferred or non-acceptable words, phrases, and forms of address than in the home. The language used in school by teachers is closer to the more formal register of writing. It is closer to the variety used by the BBC in its news bulletins and other programmes when the aim is to inform rather than to entertain. This variety is associated with a distinctive accent, originally called RP, 'Received Pronunciation', (see Trudgill, 1975). Schools must help children acquire this register as it is so often, whether we like it or not, the gateway to further education and thence to an array of careers and professions. Again I must emphasise that this does not imply that one dialect or register from any one geographical area or social class is inferior to another as far as we know, but that one variety is more *appropriate* in some social settings than another. For further reading of the above topics see Gregory and Carroll, (1978) and O'Donnell and Todd, (1980).

Appropriateness

Given that there are a number of different distinguishable varieties of English, then one of the major language development tasks will be to develop children's awareness of differences, and their ability to switch from one variety to another, according to the demands of the language situation. To become aware of this appropriateness, and to have the ability to switch language variety accordingly, is a major area of growth in children's language development.

The appropriateness of the language variety to the situation is one of the factors that may help us understand, in part, why some children apear to be virtually dumb when they are in the classroom, yet are quite vociferous in the street or playground. There may be many other causes, of course, but the effects of this implicit requirement to change from one variety to another may have been greatly underestimated. Teachers are often faced with problems of this kind. What is more, parents cannot understand why their normally talkative youngster is now reported to be inarticulate. Given the considerable differences that often exist between the variety of language used by the school and that used by children at home or in the playground, the position becomes more understandable, and, once understood, more amenable to sympathetic handling in class. Wade (1979), for example, emphasises:

> the need to look for the causes of *maladjustment* not only in the pupil and his psychological background, but also in his peer group and in the school as an institution of learning. It follows that in normal and special schools we should give careful attention to the curriculum, to teachers' attitudes *and to the use of language in learning.* (my italics)

Differences of dialect and register are, of course, only one of the factors that are at play in the reception classroom, but it is worth bearing in mind since its effects may be more extensive than we sometimes appreciate. It is, in addition, a sensitive area having connotations of social class and 'not talkin' proper'. It should be stressed that this problem needs constant appraisal throughout schooling, as some extensions of register are related to growing social awareness which is particularly apparent during adolescence. Much can be done however to attune children to register differences and to develop their sensitivity to appropriateness through the skilful use of drama.

To illustrate the extent of language variety switching that is demanded of most children in a school-home-recreational setting, the Open University Language Development team made a film of the demands made on the language repertoire of a teenage girl (O.U. T.V. Programme No. 7. PE232 1979). In this film we meet Sharon, a fifteen-year-old girl, at home (a public house), then in various school contexts where her role constantly changes.

It becomes quite clear to the viewer of the film that part of the adjustment to the various social settings in which Sharon finds herself is her ability to produce that variety of language that is most fitting for that situation. The film demonstrates that in an ordinary day most school children have to switch their language across a number of varieties which differ sometimes only in subtle ways. You might find this film a useful discussion starter with older children when dealing with appropriateness in your language work.

Idiolect

To complete the picture we need to add a third category to dialect and register, that of idiolect. Perhaps it ought to have been mentioned first as dialect diversity begins with the individual. As O'Donnell and Todd (1980, page 27) put it:

> For though most of us are unaware of the fact, or alternatively choose to ignore it, no two of us speak exactly the same language. This is so whatever language we claim to speak: each one of us has his own personal dialect, or 'idiolect' as it is called.

The dominating characteristic appears to be habitual usage of certain language features according to personal preference. One of the best-known examples of idiolect is the Spoonerism or transposition of initial consonants (e.g. 'tasting two worms' for 'wasting two terms'). There is also the habitual use of phrases such as 'Whether you like it or not', or 'If I've told him once, I've told him a hundred times' (see O'Donnell and Todd (1980 p.28) for other examples). There are many such mannerisms and clichés which come under the heading idiolect, study of which, as well as providing much interest, can alert children to some of the implicit features of language and assist the development of their own usage.

The language of books

Perhaps the most important difference in variety is that between speech and writing. Again, as with the other perhaps more subtle varieties of language switching, written language has to be acquired so that the child may become a literate member of society. If you doubt the extent of the difference, just tape-record yourself speaking on a topic and then write about the same topic and compare the two. Recently, evidence for a 'literary dialect' has been advanced by Richek (1978) who claims that some sentences are 'peculiarly literary in style and . . . taken together, form a "literary dialect" that characterises written prose.' Her study is valuable for teachers if her findings can be substantiated. I would certainly agree intuitively that some children might experience a great deal more difficulty with literary than with non-literary forms. Here is an extract from the study to illustrate the differences claimed. The examples of the different literary structures were also varied for frequency/infrequency of vocabulary.

Literary structures: frequent vocabulary
> The boy was not unkind to his sister
> To win the race she ran very fast

Literary structures: infrequent vocabulary
> The boy was not unappreciative of his sister
> To triumph in the contest, she raced very rapidly

Non-literary structures: frequent vocabulary
> The boy heard the girl singing in the next room
> He was sad that he lost the race

Non-literary structures: infrequent vocabulary
> The boy noticed the girl reciting in the next room
> He was disappointed that he failed in the contest

From a practitioner's point of view there certainly seems to be a literary dialect or register as we would prefer to call it, and thus many children have to be taught it as a variation from both their own local (geographical) dialect and the register of the home.

We must be careful, however, not to take these differences too far. In a recent article Halliday (1978a), for example, makes it clear that while we think of written and spoken language as being different, we need to be aware that 'the difference is one of degree'. He writes, 'I am far from wishing to suggest that spoken and written language are separate, discrete phenomena. They are both manifestations of the same underlying system.' He goes on, 'The difference between speech and writing is actually an instance of a more general phenomenon of variation in language, that of register.' He makes the point that I have made about appropriateness, that is, that language varies according to situation, and that much of secondary education is concerned with becoming sensitive to different registers. However, with the younger child in the initial stages of schooling the written/spoken dichotomy is the critical one. We need to be clear that the language of books and of writing is another variety of English differing from spoken language, for the latter, as we saw in Chapter 2, has an implicit context shared by the speaker and hearer. Halliday (1978a) quotes Abercrombie's words,

> The whole object of written language is to be free of any immediate context, whether personal or situational and that is why it dispenses with systematic indication of intonation and rhythm, only giving the vaguest hints in the form of question marks, commas and so on.

We have to appreciate that some of the meaning of the actual words we use in message exchanges will reside in the situation itself and not only in the words and sentences we use. For example, we may refer to 'that' table or 'that' person over 'there'. The identity of these, that is 'the actual table' and 'person' in question and their position relative to the speaker/hearer will be implicit in the situation. But notice it is extra-linguistic, some of the meaning resides outside the actual words being used. There is no need to spell the detail out in speech situations for the meaning is clear to both speakers or, if not, it can be explained. In the written situation, however, the writer has to build up the context, and replace some of the extra-linguistic meaning for the reader. In doing this he still takes a great deal of the speech situation for granted, leaving the reader to make many inferences. The language of the book is also more formal, more appropriate than that of the speech situation. Many teachers have used and are still using techniques derived from Breakthrough to Literacy (Mackay et al., 1978) to introduce their pupils to the written word. This seems to work quite well for many children but we should be aware that when children are asked to tell their teacher what it is they wish to have written down, the teacher often subtly 'translates' the spoken message of the individual child into the written register. To make this point quite clear, the reader is again asked to try transcribing speech from a tape-recording and notice how great the differences really are, and indeed how much has to be learned of transcribing systems in order to get an accurate record of speech down on to paper, for the grammar of speech is much more complex than we sometimes imagine (Halliday, 1978a).

Some characeristics of literacy in the home

Some parents, long before school and while the child is acquiring his or her first language, are intuitively aware of the child's need for language and provide a rich literary background which gives the child a flying start in school. Moon and Wells (1979) for instance have shown that 'attainment in reading at age 7 was found to be strongly predicted by knowledge of literacy on entry to school, and this in turn to be predicted by parental interest in literacy and quality of verbal interaction with the child in the pre-school years.' These parents use every opportunity to talk to and with the child even before the child can respond by word or gesture. As we will see, it appears to be important for the child to be able, for example, to tune in to the intonation patterns of speech from the beginning, and to do this the child needs to be surrounded by language in the natural setting of the home.

As soon as their children respond to or understand language, many parents begin to teach them nursery rhymes and tell them simple stories. The child becomes aware of the shape and form of the rhyme and story in the natural, warm, supportive environment of the family. Stories are not only told but read to the child who will begin to follow the story in the book. The child will thus be introduced gradually to the language of books and to the written code. The black squiggles on the page come to have meaning, they contain the story, they 'speak' the same language.

In this fashion the child from a home which provides a rich language background will have had an uninterrupted natural progression from the acquisition of his or her first language, through to what we are concerned with in the development stages at school with no formal instruction and no drill. These children are fortunate because they are constantly learning, during informal situations, that the language of the book is akin to the spoken variety, but with some significant differences.

It may come as a surprise to some teachers to learn that many children do not understand the basic relationship between speech and writing. 'A child who is learning to read and write already knows language in its spoken form; but he does not know he knows it.' (Halliday, 1978a).

Looking at similar problems in further detail Ferreiro (1978) reported that:

children who cannot yet read (in the conventional sense) nevertheless have very precise ideas about what can be found in a written text. They do not deal with the different parts of a sentence in the same manner: at first children do not expect the verb to be written; then the verb is graphically represented, but articles are not. Acquiring knowledge about the writing system is a cognitive process.

Downing (1979) has made a lengthy study of the importance of cognitive clarity and learning to read. In a way it may be important for some children to become used to school language first, for this has some features in common with book language, and so can serve as an introduction.

Intonation

Another component of language that has been taken for granted and not received enough attention over the years is the development of children's ability to fully master pitch or intonation, that quality of speech that conveys meaning and yet, although closely related, is distinct from words and their order in sentences (see Halliday, 1978a). It has been noticed that children's use of intonation begins very early in language acquisition. If you are fortunate enough to be able to 'listen in' to mother and baby communication, you will find that very early in life babies are excellent mimics of pitch patterns (Cruttenden, 1979). The child is, as it were, tuning in to the intonation patterns of the mother and copying her. If you listen very carefully you will be able to detect the rising and falling 'tunes' – the technical term for the rise and fall of the sounds – of the mother and often you will hear the baby echoing them. There is no indication that the baby is doing anything but mimicking its mother at eight months, but these tunes are related to the basic melodies of the English tongue and perhaps help the child to divide the stream of sound into meaningful chunks (Karmiloff-Smith, 1977).

Intonation patterns continue for many years to be 'picked up' (the expression is used deliberately, for children are very rarely taught intonation patterns formally). You will have noticed that we convey, emphasise, confirm, and establish the continuity of some of our intended meanings by means of intonation (Halliday and Hasan, 1976). You may have come across the example that has been used in nursery or infant schools (see TV Programme 1, OU Course PE232) where a child of about 4½ years of age is asked to judge whether all the contents of a bag (e.g. toys, sweets) have been taken out, by the intonation used for the final article. Some children soon detect the intonation and can predict whether the bag is empty or not; some are not able to tell as they are not yet able to follow the tune or are not able to connect the intonation pattern with the intended meaning of the event.

Another example comes from the reading of football scores (Cruttenden, 1974). Here boys are particularly good at judging whether a team has won, lost or drawn from the intonation of the reader of the scores. A useful demonstration of this for children is to leave out the actual numerical score and read the rest out, asking them to fill in the results. This can be done later in the junior school when at ten or eleven years you will find that some children can so manipulate intonation that they are able to read the same passage in different ways so as to alter the whole meaning of the passage.

It is clear that the ability to cope with intonation to the extent where it can be consciously manipulated in this way has been developing over the years. This does not seem to have been taught much in schools, even though it is one aspect of language that an infant begins to acquire before he learns to talk, and children continue to pick up the intonation patterns associated with English until they are at least ten or eleven years old. They have been learning this informally and without being able to verbalise what is happening. Older children 'know' that it is not only words and groupings of words that convey meaning but also the intonation patterns that accompany them.

We should note from this that the very process of reading aloud, particularly in the early stages, requires children to restore the intonation patterns of speech as part of the process of decoding the words from the print. They need to use both the meaning of the language and the graphic cues in the text before them to perform this activity.

Perera (1979) states that intonation has three main functions in speech:

1 It indicates the grammatical structure of an utterance by dividing it into grammatically relevant word-groups.

2 It is sometimes the sole means of marking the grammatical function of an utterance. For example, *You've finished* is marked in speech as a statement by a falling tone and as a question by a rising tone.

3 It conveys the attitude of the speaker. For example, *You are clever* may express grudging admiration, in which case it will have an intonation pattern like this: *You'are^vclever*; or it may express heavy

sarcasm, in which case it will have a pattern like this: You ₐare clever.

In writing, intonation is not expressed directly so these three functions have to be fulfilled in other ways:

1 Grammatical structure: punctuation marks are used to indicate some structural units. Sentence boundaries are marked by full stops, question marks and exclamation marks; smaller grammatically relevant word-groups are not so systematically delineated. For example, although adverbials at the beginning of a sentence are frequently separated from the rest of the sentence by a comma (e.g. *Nevertheless, I shan't go*), many complex sentences have no internal punctuation marks to indicate their structure, e.g. *A doctor John Brown knew bought the car.* The grammatical structure of this sentence is immediately apparent in speech but is perhaps less clear in writing.

2 Sentence function: statements are marked by full stops, questions by question marks and exclamations by exclamation marks. Commands with the grammatical form of imperatives (with no expressed subject) end with a full stop if they are calm in tone e.g. ⟨*Be careful.*⟩ represents *Be ₍careful,* and with an exclamation mark if the tone is excited e.g. ⟨*Be careful!*⟩represents *Be˅careful.* Commands with the grammatical form of questions end with a question mark if they are polite or tentative, e.g. *Would you shut the door?,* and with an exclamation mark if they are forceful, e.g. *Will you go away!*

3 Speaker's attitude: this is very difficult to convey in writing. O'Connor and Arnold (1973) comment, 'One measure of a writer's success is his ability to solve the problem of suggesting the exact meaning he has in mind even though he has no direct method of conveying intonation.'

So the written symbols do not represent speech but only some aspects of it. As we have seen, the situational features of speech in particular are not present in writing and as a result, the two are very different. In most cases this application of intonation pattern is done with very little formal teaching of the language relationships involved. For further reading on intonation see Bolinger, D. (1972) and on reading and intonation, Brazil, et al. (1980).

There is, of course, the fact that teachers often provide models of oral reading and some may draw attention to the punctuation marks, demonstrating how, for instance, the voice rises to indicate a question. But notice again, the reader has to realise from the meaning of the passage what the appropriate intonation pattern is, probably before the question mark comes into peripheral vision. In some ways the question mark confirms the question, rather than indicates it, for to read fluently aloud requires the ability to begin the appropriate intonation pattern before the question mark is perceived.

Language awareness

Before I go on to outline other neglected or unnoticed features of language, one cognitive aspect closely associated with language development, namely linguistic awareness, needs mentioning.

Mattingly (1972) discussed linguistic awareness and reading and in doing so quoted Liberman's remark that 'reading is parasitic on language'. Mattingly (p.145) elaborated this notion remarking that:

> Reading is seen not as a parallel activity in the visual mode to speech perception in the auditory mode; there are differences between the two activities that cannot be explained in terms of the differences of modality. They can be explained only if we regard reading as a deliberately acquired, language-based skill, dependent upon the speaker-hearer's awareness of certain aspects of primary linguistic activity (primary here means speaking and listening). By virtue of this linguistic awareness, written text initiates the synthetic linguistic process common to both reading and speech, enabling the reader to get the writer's message and so to recognize what has been written. (my parenthesis)

Mattingly (p. 140) also mentions the extent of individual variation in linguistic awareness. Of this he says,

> Some speaker-hearers are not only very conscious of linguistic patterns but exploit their consciousness with obvious pleasure in verbal play (e.g. punning) or verbal work (e.g. linguistic analysis). Others seem never to be aware of much more than words and are surprised when quite obvious linguistic patterns are pointed out to them.

During the primary years children are increasingly able to 'step outside' their normal use of language and become observers of their own language. Although this facility may have been present since first language acquisition (Weir, 1962), it does become obvious that between seven and eight years, children's interest in language as an entity in itself begins to flourish. Indeed, Sinclair de Swatz (1971) suggests that changes in thinking around the age of six or seven lead to new forms of verbal behaviour. Reporting this, Lundberg (1980, p.87) goes on to state that 'a general capacity for detachment paves the way for metalinguistic reflection, as well as the ability to find different verbal formulations describing the same event.' The use of the term metalinguistic is used here as an equivalent term to linguistic awareness.

Many primary teachers remark on their children's growing awareness of homonymous words, for example, words which can sound the same but have different meanings, e.g. duck (bird) and duck (lower one's head or body); or, though sounding the same and having different meanings, are spelt differently, e.g. tale (story) and tail (appendage). These homophones, as they are called, are unambiguous when written down but are potentially ambiguous in speech. Homonymy does allow us the doubtful joys of punning and children are noted for their enthusiasm for word play and riddles as they become aware of the potential of homonymy. If we conceive language development as being a continuum, children begin to take a delight in playing with words, punning, and savouring jokes that rely on word play, as they advance towards the mastery the adult language user has. Language teaching becomes more effective once this stage of linguistic awareness is reached.

This awareness of language, while marking a cognitive advance as well as a linguistic one – the two are interactive, is also a characteristic of the nature of language development. The origins of the 'fun' of language can be found for example, in the earlier savouring of nursery rhymes and the delight of poetry and songs. This in turn might be seen as a continuation of the experimentation with the spectator role of language that Weir (1962) observed in the crib.

Thematisation

Another characteristic of language that has not received the attention in education it deserves, and which assumes greater importance as the child proceeds along the developmental continuum towards the level of literacy required by present day living, is the ability to recognise the theme or thread of a piece of writing or written discourse.

If you think about this, you soon realise from our earlier discussion of the subtle linguistic factors at work in some home and school environments, that children who have had a rich diet of stories have absorbed in passing the highly predictable nature of their structure. More often than not stories begin with standard introductory phrases such as 'Once upon a time . . .', 'One day in a far off land . . .', 'I remember once some time ago . . .' and so on. You will be aware from the many examples you have experienced that, when you encounter such 'openers', you begin to predict the shape of structure of the discourse that follows. You will 'know' from the many stories you have heard that such an opening signals not only the beginning of a story but also a series of predictable features within that story. You will anticipate that next the scene will be set and the characters introduced. You will expect that the characters for whom your sympathies will have been aroused will enter upon some adventure which will ascend to a climax or a series of lesser emphases. Children become intimately involved with their favourite stories and no matter how many times they have heard the story, will be caught up with the adventures as they unfold and, it is important to notice, their predictability. They will 'know' that the situation will be resolved, wrongs righted, and the wording of the ending of the story will be eagerly anticipated: 'and they lived happily ever after'. Many of you may have tried to divert the story ever so little and have been upbraided for your presumption. The anticipation is so strong that the very words have to be identical from telling to telling. Predictions are made and a great deal of the satisfaction results from having them constantly confirmed. As a result of this anticipation, children have absorbed, through similar cues in other situations where language is used, the abstract features of a theme, or as Grimes (1975) has it, 'the thread of discourse'. The story has, of course, a long tradition, at one time being the basis for the oral transmission of the history of the tribe from one generation to another (Pellowski, 1977). It is still one of the most engaging forms of communication and a powerful attention holder. More often than not, this informed language teaching with story-telling as its medium is introduced and developed within the natural language environment provided by the literate home.

Applebee (1978) has shown how the child's concept of story grows with the years. He demonstrates that children even as young as two years old use some of the conventions of the story mode; and that children as old as six years do not distinguish fact from fiction. This lack of differentiation between fact and fiction and its late development is important in overall cognitive growth, but for our purposes we should note that 'the stories they hear help them to acquire expectation about what the world is like – its vocabulary and syntax as well as its people and places – without the distracting pressure of separating the real from the make-believe.'

Those children who have had these early introductions to literacy will bring such implicit knowledge of the story format to the school situation as part of their general linguistic awareness. It will be reinforced in the early years at school as children move on to their first reading books, which will often be found to contain many of those same familiar traditional stories. They will use, without instruction, that implicit thematic knowledge to help unlock the language from printed code and thence to re-create the story.

Children who have had experience of story themes at home will need to have those underlying relationships brought to the surface for examination when they come to school. How this is done will depend a great deal on individual differences, which will vary widely according to the experiences of the children in the group being taught. A useful exercise during early reading practice is that of predicting what will happen next in the story ('group prediction'). This will play its part in an overall approach to reading that is meaning-directed.

Schools usually provide a rich diet of stories for children, but the story or narrative is not the only type of text in existence. Children need to read texts that vary considerably from the story format and the structure of these texts will often be unfamiliar. There are some five different types of literary texts given by Werlich (1976). These are description, narrative, exposition, argumentation, and instruction. As children progress through their schooling, these different text types will come their way, often in a haphazard fashion and with little or no introduction to their differences and how they should be read. It is thus difficult for young secondary school readers who have only recently mastered the code-cracking process in the junior and infant school to have to cope with texts of differing types, and with the absence of the story structure with which they have become familiar. Thus predictability and its influence on word recognition will be missing also and reading, in many of these cases will not be as fluent as it might be.

Frames and schema; word meaning and concept development

In this chapter so far we have drawn attention to a number of language and language-related factors that have been taken for granted or whose importance has been underestimated or neglected during reading instruction. Another such factor in this same category is closely concerned with the basic symbolic nature of language.

Children learn quickly and easily in their early years to name objects and persons. The sounds they learn are symbols for the actual thing or person to whom they wish to refer, for that is the nature of symbols (Brown, 1958). The process is, however, not quite as straightforward as we sometimes imagine, for the naming or symbolic process can be misleading or extended beyond its actual validity. The word can be uttered and used correctly in context, yet the child's concept for which the word is a symbol may not be as advanced as adults may assume. Often, unless our attention is drawn to this possibility, we assume that, when a child has used the word correctly in context, it carries the same meaning for the child as for us. But this may not be so. Take a well-known example: the word 'tree' can in certain contexts refer to all the trees in nature or to one special familiar tree, the oak or ash. However, consider the young reader in a city-centre, urban environment whose experience of trees has been restricted to the stunted variety at the foot of a block of high-rise flats or at the boundary of a playground. Contrast this with the richly developed concept of 'tree' that a teacher might have. It is not uncommon for such a teacher to have visited an arboretum and to have seen a great variety of trees. The word used by the child and the teacher is the same but the concept conveyed could be widely disparate. This potential for mismatch has considerable implications for the way adults communicate with children, for we cannot transfer the concept that we have to the child with one or several words. The concept will need many experiences, both actual and verbal, to become mature. Now transfer this insight to the reading situation. The reading of a word aloud, its recognition in print and its sounding, does not mean that the concept it carries for the child will necessarily enable it to be comprehended in the totality of the reading passage. It is true that from the rest of the context the reader may extend the original concept, but it would be unwise to allow reading aloud to be a criterion for reading progress, let alone the results of a graded word reading test. The teacher should not assume when the words are sounded correctly that comprehension, in terms of the concepts adults have acquired, is at the same level for the child as it is for them.

There is a further point which Donaldson (1978) makes in her book *Children's Minds* which relates well to the development of word meaning. Referring to production and understanding, she points out that care needs to be taken as it is not always true that comprehension precedes production. 'He understands a lot more than he says.' When speaking or writing children can choose those words with which they are confident and familiar but when receiving (comprehending), someone other than the listener or reader is choosing the words. The child has no choice but to attempt to comprehend them. In the reading situation, the author chooses the words and the reader has to understand what the author provides. The reader is not free to choose only those words he or she can read. And yet elements of the concepts carried by the word can be gained from the context in reading. That is, if reading is taught as an active reconstruction process.

We have looked now at some factors which have perhaps not had the attention they deserve: the varieties of the English language including the language of books, and register switching required of children by the situations in which they find themselves; intonation; the theme of a story, the staging of prose, the different types of texts presented to children to read, and internalised language or conscious awareness of language.

Beyond the sentence

One recent development, which will doubtless have considerable influence on the study of reading, has come about by some linguists beginning to work systematically with units of language larger than the sentence. For many years, as was intimated in Chapter 2, the largest unit of language to be studied by most university linguists in Britain and America was the sentence. Chomsky (1957), for example, based his influential theory on the structure of sentences, or to be more precise, syntactical structures. There were, however, some linguists who contemplated longer units. Kenneth Pike (1964), the American linguist, for example, wrote:

> A bias of mine – not shared by many linguists – is the conviction that beyond the sentence lie grammatical structures available to linguistic analysis describable by technical procedures, and usable by the author for the generation of the literary works through which he reports to us his observations.

Few followed this 'bias' by a methodical study of those 'grammatical structures beyond the sentence' until a decade later and then mostly on another continent. This resistance to the idea of going beyond the sentence as a unit of study has been most marked among American and British linguists. European linguists have a long tradition of working with longer stretches of language. Concentration on the sentence would seem to have a lengthy history too, for as long ago as 1751, the philosophical grammarian James Harris, in his treatise *Hermes*, wrote:

> The longest extension, with which Grammar has to do, is the extension here considered, that is to say, a sentence. The great extensions (such as Syllogisms, Paragraphics, Sections and complete works) belong not to Grammar, but to Arts of higher order; not to mention that all of them are but sentences repeated. (quoted in Hendricks, 1976)

This, of course, tends to equate linguists with grammarians, and this is too clear-cut a distinction, as we have seen in Chapter 2. Those who study style, poetics, rhetoric, and narrative theory might well call themselves linguists and they have certainly demonstrated over the years that there are regularities, amounting to rules, in stretches of language composed of more than one sentence, but there is, as yet, no generally agreed satisfactory grammar, traditional, descriptive or generative of units 'beyond' the sentence.

In Britain, however, one work that looks at the properties of texts from a global perspective stands out. This is the work of Halliday and Hasan (1976) who supply an inventory of those linguistic mechanisms that create cohesion (or unity) in texts. This characteristic of cohesion is said to bind the text together into a whole meaningful unit. It is such an important language feature in relation to reading that it will form the basis of the next four chapters.

In many ways the developments mentioned earlier in relation to cohesion are beginning to have a revitalising effect on the study and teaching of reading, for there can be little doubt that semantic considerations (i.e. those concerned with meaning) are not restricted to individual sentences nor are the pragmatic or intentional characteristics. They are contained, more often than not, in the interrelationship of sequences of sentences. After all, we read to gain meaning from the whole of the text, not just its individual sentences and it is for the most part the gist of what we read that remains with us.

This has considerable significance for education, for when we are thinking about the process of re-creating a message from either sound or print, we are dealing mostly with explanations or descriptions that are of some length. It usually takes a few pages at least to convey an educational concept or to explain a natural phenomenon. Even simple stories written for the very young consist of many sentences. Teachers are more likely to be interested in the meaning conveyed by the whole passage of print, rather than individual sentences. Furthermore, as education proceeds for the child, the texts chosen for the subject or content areas of the curriculum contain increasingly lengthy passages.

Teachers, then, will not find the concept of the global nature of texts strange, for children's comprehension of what they have read, and their own writing, depend on an appreciation of these unifying factors. In their day-to-day work, teachers are used to looking at children's writing as whole pieces of work. They will often, perhaps, assess a child's written contribution and award a grade or mark of some kind for the totality of that piece of work. Teachers are called upon to make these judgements daily. Usually, while acknowledging the quality of the components that go to make up the whole, they can award a grade for the piece of work without undue difficulty.

In this way teachers judge work by the extent to which its parts 'hang together'. Furthermore, teachers are able to advise their pupils how to rearrange their compositions so as to improve the cohesion and flow of their work. It follows, then, that teachers know whether one piece of work is more cohesive than another and what alterations will improve it.

Most adults are able to do the same with reading texts. Try reading this passage. It contains the same sentences as the original but the sequences have been jumbled. After reading them rearrange the sentences as you think the author intended. Check your version with the original on page 136. Try to specify which words made the linkages between sentences apparent to you.

1. The workers hastily conferred with the foreman. 2. On a recent sunny afternoon in Athens workers were burrowing down some distance from the Acropolis, seeking the bedrock for the foundation of a new building. 3. He telephoned the site's owner who, as required by law, notified the Antiquities Department. 4. They were being watched by the normal complement of roadside super-

intendents shouting occasional words of advice. 5. A quick inspection by an expert from the Antiquities Department established that the site was worth investigating. 6. Instead of bedrock, the workmen had unearthed what appeared to be large slabs of smooth limestone. 7. Arrangements were made for sifting through the earth of the excavation next day. 8. The building workers departed. 9. Suddenly, the digging stopped. 10. A guard was posted.

It is relatively easy to establish by simple tasks, such as the re-assembling of texts, that skilled readers have acquired the ability to discriminate between texts of different levels of cohesion. Barnard (1974) in a doctoral dissertation demonstrated this property of cohesion by getting his subjects to reconstruct a passage from a set of scrambled sentences in much the same way as you have done. The more subjects that recreated a passage, the more cohesive the passage was deemed to be. In other words textual cohesion was not established theoretically as in the Halliday and Hasan work which we mentioned earlier and will go on to examine in detail, but as a product of the judgements of students. Barnard showed, therefore, that the quality of cohesion was detectable and that it could be said to be present to a greater or lesser extent.

That there is a global characteristic present in texts is undeniable, but its is only very recently that linguists have explored systematically the detail of the linguistic features that give texts this quality. Some of these features may appear new and some quite familiar, but the perspective as a whole gives us a new dimension along which to base our teaching.

We have seen above that texts have qualities that an adult skilled reader can detect. For a text to be recognised as a text rather than a haphazard collection of sentences, it must have an orderly and cohesive construction. It follows from this that there must be ways in which the sentences that compose such a text are linked. These order arrangements, or sentence sequences, will serve to integrate the text and together provide the cohesion we can detect. This being so it is pertinent for teachers of reading to know more about the ability skilled readers have to perceive these factors. For it follows that this ability must have been acquired in some way, and what is more, by a process that has not, as far as we are aware, been directly taught. In some secondary schools there have always been studies of style, stylistics and poetics and some of these text linguistic features will have been examined, but there has been little direct teaching concerned with the ways in which texts cohere, either to help children read them or construct them.

Summary

We have noted that much of the work done in schools during the years of compulsory schooling is dependent upon children's developing language ability. Furthermore, we have noted that many factors concerning that language ability have not been taught but have remained implicit. Amongst such factors are language variety, including the language of books, the register of instruction, the theme of a story and different types of text and cohesion. These features all have direct bearing on reading. These text linguistic factors will become more intricate in the texts presented to older children as the content presented in textbooks becomes more adult in kind. Children will undoubtedly need the continuity of specific reading instruction if they are to achieve the standards society is now demanding.

4 Cohesive ties: the reference system

This chapter contains details of how the linguistic mechanisms appear to work and the main elements of the reference system of ties.

We have said that linguists in Britain, America, and especially on the continent of Europe, have recently begun to give us new insights into the organisation of units of language larger than the sentence. The linguistic features involved have begun to be systematically explored and several systems advanced. One such set of proposals has been provided by Halliday and Hasan (1976). In their study of the properties of texts, which we will follow, they explore the nature of textual cohesion and identify ways in which it is achieved.

The basic concept they propose in their book, *Cohesion in English*, is that of the cohesive tie. This concept is attractive not only for the way in which it establishes the basic notion of tying parts of a text together but also for its great potential as a tangible teaching technique. It is a way of dealing concretely with an otherwise difficult abstract concept. That it lends itself to becoming a practical teaching approach is a bonus. It gives teachers and, through them, their pupils a notion that they can readily understand – the concept of tying things together by means of suitable knots.

Anaphora

This same property is true of cohesive ties, for cohesion in texts is achieved by a series of linguistic linking mechanisms that, like knots, are used for particular purposes. For instance, some teachers of reading are familiar with 'backward acting cues', those linkages (such as pronouns) that a reader must negotiate in order to become fluent. Such cues are examples of a syntactical relationship which linguists call 'anaphora'. This device is often used in texts as it is one of the basic ways of relating one part of a sentence with another and, what is just as important in this context, linking sentences. Look at the way in which the pronoun 'he' is used as a very simple linking device in the following sentences.

The electrician found the fault and began to repair the power cable.

When he had finished he went back to the depot.

Here the simple pronoun 'he' relates to electrician, linking two actions performed by the same person. 'He' refers back anaphorically to 'electrician'. Many such devices are used but we do not notice them until our attention is drawn to them by ambiguity or mis-understanding. How children learn to cope with them is not clearly understood, but we must assume that what they know has been implicitly learned as language develops.

Anaphoric chains
Some of the ties are much more complex than the above example, interweaving and spanning longer stretches of text. Look, for instance, at the chaining and resulting cohesion provided by the various anaphoric relationships boxed thus [ ] in the following letter to The Times (over page). Remember that we are looking at some of the reference group of ties only in this instance. There are many others acting simultaneously as the letter is being read.

In his letter to The Times, Mr Evers assumes, among other things, prior knowledge of writers (and letters to The Times), the ways in which scientific paradigms are generated, those recognised as being traditional scientists and those presenting pseudo-scientific entertainment.

At the outset the reader meets two names, Levin (1) and Inglis (2), followed by the pronoun 'him' (3). Here there is a minor ambiguity for the reader. Which is the intended antecedent, Levin or Inglis? It is usual to make the link with the nearest name, here Inglis, but a case could be made for relating back directly to Levin. Compare, however, 'his' (33) referring back to Levin (31) and not Ayer (32) which is the nearer.

The next proper name, Kuhn, may be known to some readers of The Times and any relevant information about his work would improve the general understanding of Mr Evers' letter as a whole. The possessive pronoun 'his' (5) links, in a simple direct way, the author and the book which is concerned with scientific paradigms (6), an important theme of the letter. Notice now the effect of the

Figure 4. Examples of anaphoric chaining

Letter to *The Times*　　　13th January, 1978
Explaining Psychic Effects　　From I.D. Evers

Sir,

1.

Mr Levin's comments (January 6) about Brian Inglis's **2.**

3.

book *Natural and Supernatural*, do not do him credit.

The achievement of today's science are not the result

of accepting strange events as supernatural but of

always searching for a rational explanation.

4.　　**5.**

Kuhn, in his book *The Structure of Scientific Revolutions*

6.

has shown how and why the scientific paradigms, i.e. the

theories, models and procedures employed by scientists

7.

at any time are very powerful. They cannot be overthrown

by a motley collection of unconnected observations of

8.

events which seem to contradict them When Mr Levin **9.**

10.

implies that these happenings cannot be explained as

fakes, hallucinations, chance, etc., or by powers and

senses already known to be possessed by human beings,

11.

he is dogmatically begging the question at issue.

12.

Perhaps they can be thus explained, perhaps not.

13.　　　　　　　**14.**

Until we can be absolutely sure that they cannot be

15.

explained with the help of knowledge and theories we

16.

have so far, we must employ Occam's razor and not make

17.

unnecessary assumptions. Where neglect of this

principle can lead is shown by the example of the

18.

books of von Daneken, who finds it necessary to postu-

late visits by extraterrestrial beings to explain　　　TO 24.

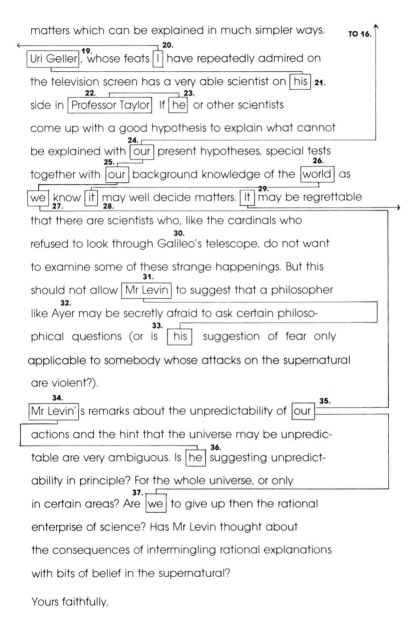

matters which can be explained in much simpler ways. TO 16.

Uri Geller, whose feats I have repeatedly admired on

the television screen has a very able scientist on his

side in Professor Taylor If he or other scientists

come up with a good hypothesis to explain what cannot

be explained with our present hypotheses, special tests

together with our background knowledge of the world as

we know it may well decide matters. It may be regrettable

that there are scientists who, like the cardinals who

refused to look through Galileo's telescope, do not want

to examine some of these strange happenings. But this

should not allow Mr Levin to suggest that a philosopher

like Ayer may be secretly afraid to ask certain philoso-

phical questions (or is his suggestion of fear only

applicable to somebody whose attacks on the supernatural

are violent?).

Mr Levin's remarks about the unpredictability of our

actions and the hint that the universe may be unpredic-

table are very ambiguous. Is he suggesting unpredict-

ability in principle? For the whole universe, or only

in certain areas? Are we to give up then the rational

enterprise of science? Has Mr Levin thought about

the consequences of intermingling rational explanations

with bits of belief in the supernatural?

Yours faithfully,

I.D. Evers.   24, Priory Road, Edgbaston, Birmingham

pronouns, 'They' (7) and 'them' (8). These simple pronouns keep the theme of scientific paradigms alive across the sentence boundary. Interwoven within these pronouns, the name Levin (9) is mentioned again as though to remind the reader that it is his comments that are the point of the letter. Then 'He' (11) refers back anaphorically over the intervening 25 words adding a further comment as to Levin's dogmatism. A further chain begins with 'these happenings' (10) followed by 'they' (12) and 'they' (14) linking over two sentences and a paragraph.

At the beginning of the third paragraph the reader meets what is called an exophoric 'we' (13) which is not cohesive. The letter writer is, as it were, referring outside the text, speaking for all the readers who have knowledge of this topic. This 'we' (13) is reiterated by 'we' (15) and again at 'we' (16) and now provides a cohesive effect. The mention of Occam's razor (17) would mean a great deal to those with prior knowledge of parsimony in theory construction as would familiarity with von Daneken's (18) book on extraterrestrial beings.

Note next that the pronoun 'I' (20) refers to the letter writer, and although readers need not know his actual name to understand his letter, they will be aware from their background knowledge of this type of text (letters to a newspaper) that his identity will be found at the top and bottom of the letter. The pronoun 'our' (24) is related to the 'we' chain (13), (15) and (16) in the previous paragraph and is linked to 'our' (25) then 'we' (27) and later to 'our' (35) and 'we' (37) in the final paragraph.

Other anaphoric references occur alongside and within those that are chained across longer stretches of text: 'world' (26), for example, is referred to by 'it' (28). Yet, 'It' (29) at the beginning of the very next sentence is an anticipatory subject which is not anaphoric but refers forward to the statement that 'there are scientists who . . . do not want to examine some of these strange happenings.'

For the identity of 'his' (33), it is necessary to go back to Levin (31) and not in this case to the nearest name, Ayer (32). (Cf. 'him' (3) with Levin (1) and Inglis (2) above.) Again, 'he' (36) refers back to Levin (34) across a sentence boundary.

It may come as a surprise to find seemingly simple words, like those in the pronoun system in English, performing such important tasks. And indeed to the skilled reader the processing of chains of cohesive ties, maintaining a theme for example, is virtually automatic. Yet when this is set against the level of prior knowledge demanded by the writer, a difficult reading task will ensue for some readers. This elaborate web of chained connections is a characteristic of the language we use and the extent of this intricacy is usually left implicit during language teaching. What we have seen above, however, is only part of the cohesion in texts to be negotiated when we read.

Consider for a moment young readers who have just begun to read or older readers, who are still only reading slowly, trying to tie together these cohesive elements. We soon begin to understand how some reading problems may arise from what, at first glance, appears to be simple material. If you recall the nature of the task uncovered by this analysis, and if you consider some of the apparently simple texts presented to children in middle and secondary schools, you will soon appreciate that reading needs much more teaching support than it gets at present. It should be remembered that whilst word recognition may seem to be adequate, knowledge of what those words signal is also required for efficient reading. Some words are pluri-functional, that is, the same word can do more than one job. Note also that some of the relationships, particularly the identification of the antecedents of the pronouns, need to be kept active in memory as the passage is being read (e.g. 'we' (13), (15) and (16) refer to 'our' (24), (25) and 'we' (27); while 'our' (35) and 'we' (37) refers back over two sentences and a paragraph). This involves considerable cognitive ability, for more than one task is being carried out simultaneously. That is, the relationships are being recognised and the meaning of one sentence confirmed and related to that of another. Furthermore, the reader needs to be constantly alert, for the same pronoun may have changing referents and this is particularly so in some early reading books.

While a very simple cohesive tie, that of anaphoric pronouns, has been demonstrated, one of the most surprising things that recent research at the Open University (see Chapman, 1980b for summary) has shown, is that full understanding and ability to use the ties that go to make up textual cohesion is still being acquired well after the initial stages of learning to read. Mastery of some of the ties, as shown by cloze tests, is only achieved by some pupils late in the secondary school and yet, ironically, reading itself, unless remedial, as noted in the previous chapter, is hardly taught in later schooling.

The pronouns we have used to illustrate anaphoric relationships within texts are only one part of one of the categories of cohesive

Figure 5.   The five groups of cohesive ties

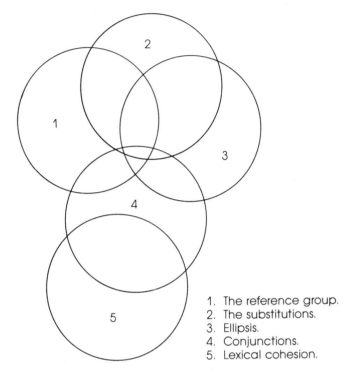

1. The reference group.
2. The substitutions.
3. Ellipsis.
4. Conjunctions.
5. Lexical cohesion.

ties identified by Halliday and Hasan who have suggested that the ties can be grouped into five main categories. These, represented in Figure 5, are the reference group, the substitutions, ellipsis, conjunctions and lexical cohesion. Reference cohesive ties, substitution and ellipsis, although they have their differences, operate in the text in a similar fashion. The full identification of a reference, substitute or elliptical item in a text relies on its relationship with a word or string of words elsewhere in the text. Lexical cohesion, on the other hand, occurs when words have relationships of a different kind, that is, a word or words is/are repeated, or have some other semantic or associative relation. The conjunctions fall between these two main groupings, sometimes linking one idea in the text with another or, if the meaning is to be inferred, acting as confirmation. These five groups of cohesive ties and their sub-groupings will be dealt with in turn.

Reference

We come now to the first of the main groupings of cohesive ties, that of reference. In any communication, we employ a variety of ways to refer to people, objects, emotions, or ideas. One of the simplest forms for instance, is naming. We give a name to a person (or thing) to distinguish that person (or thing) from any other. Thereafter, when we wish to speak about that person we refer to him, or her, simply by name. Unless a person is well known, and is thereby part of a reader's prior knowledge of the world, then an author has to tell the readers who that person is and describe his or her character and situation. In other words the author has to provide part of the context that is taken for granted in face-to-face conversation. In this way some reference items can be identified explicitly from within the text but the identification of others lies outside the text, being supplied from the reader's knowledge of the world of the particular contextual situation. Halliday and Hasan term the former (reference within the text) endophora or endophoric reference; and the latter (reference outside the text) exophora or exophoric reference.

We saw earlier when giving an illustration of a simple cohesive tie that the pronoun 'he' was identified by anaphoric reference to 'the electrician'. We interpreted 'he' by referral back to 'the electrician' and note it was not any electrician, but that particular electrician (signalled by 'the') who had repaired the power cable: the reference was explicit. In this case the reference was within the text or endophoric, whereas if we read:

'For he's a jolly good fellow
And so say all of us',

we do not know who 'he' is and we have to refer to the situation for interpretation. The reference is thus exophoric. If we read this small fragment of text from a torn newspaper report, for example, we cannot identify the 'he' from this amount of information, but to those singing the refrain there would be little doubt who 'he' was. They were within the speech situation context but the reader has to find the identity of 'he' from outside the text.

To complete the picture we should add the kind of reference, still within the text, that looks forward for its interpretation. This is called cataphora, and here is a typical example:

'Because her horse was lame Gillian had to miss the gymkhana.'

The pronoun 'her' is resolved by forward reference to Gillian. A diagram showing the relationships between exophoric, endophoric, anaphoric, and cataphoric reference is given in Figure 6.

Figure 6. Exophoric, endophoric, anaphoric, and cataphoric relations

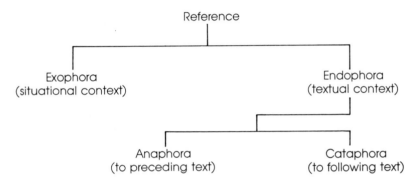

(From Halliday and Hasan 1976)

To summarise then, reference can be exophoric, relying on factors outside the text for its full interpretation. In this it does not contribute to the cohesion of the text. Endophoric reference however operates within the text itself and is thereby cohesive. Endophoric reference can be either anaphoric or cataphoric with the former being the most common.

Three types of reference cohesive ties can be distinguished, personal, demonstrative and comparative. The first of these is fairly easy to identify and using the outline of the mechanisms in Figure 7, we can see how these groupings of reference elements perform and contribute to cohesion. The linkings performed by the ties assist the reader to build up the overall meaning intended by the author. We will look at each group in some detail and note how very pervasive reference is in texts.

Figure 7. The reference group of cohesive ties

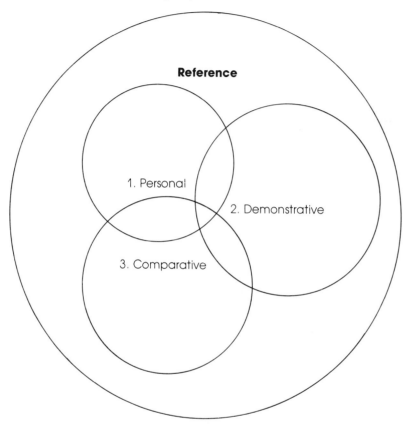

Personal Reference

We will begin by examining the first group, personal reference. Notice how the system, which contains personal pronouns, possessive adjectives and possessive pronouns, works during conversation. This part of the system assists the speaker to identify the person or persons being referred to by the role he or she is playing in the communication event. The speaker or originator of the message refers to himself as 'I', or if there is more than one, as 'we'. A speaker will refer to something he or she possesses as 'mine' and the person or persons for whom that message is intended as 'you'. This is all quite straightforward, but when we consider that the pronouns are not related to anyone in particular, but to the roles people are playing in the communication situation, then the confusion that might arise when poor or slow readers are, for example, trying to follow a conversation in print, becomes apparent. A useful way of looking at the personal reference system, then, is to analyse the set of pronouns we use by distinguishing the roles being played in a communication event. Halliday and Hasan presented such an analysis in tabular form thus:

Table 1   Pronouns analysed according to role

SPEECH ROLES			OTHER ROLES		
	Speaker	Addressee	Specific		Generalised human
			Human	Non-human	
one	I, me mine, my	you, you, yours, your	he, him, his, his	it, it (its), it.	one, one one's
			she, her, hers, her		
more than one	we, us, ours, our		they, them theirs, their		

(From Halliday and Hasan 1976, p.44)

Within natural speech situations a great deal is assumed by the speaker, who does not need to spell out every detail in order to convey his message to his hearer. The situation itself provides most of the context and therefore the cohesion. In the written situation, some of the situation has to be made explicit and some has to be inferred by the reader either from his world knowledge or knowlege of his language. Those taking part in the communication event will know something, for example, of the 'ground rules' for conversation as part of their general communicative competence (see Hymes, 1971 and Lyons, 1977). Next time you are chatting to a friend notice that you will know almost intuitively when you are expected to respond or when it is your turn to speak or, on some occasions, to stay silent. There are implicit rules to follow. And note further, in conversational situations, the pronoun 'I' moves from speaker to speaker according to role. 'I' does not refer only to the first speaker, to me, but will be used next by the addressee as he takes on the role of the speaker. It is not possible with present conventions, as we have seen in Chapter 3, to transfer all the characteristics of speech to the written form: very important features such as intonation will be missing, but the reader has to be aware of these and other features of communicative competence when reading direct speech. Often the reader has to infer the identities involved and unless correct identification is maintained the text will be difficult to comprehend fully. In an anaphoric chain, for example, the composition of a group of characters referred to by 'they' can change often, yet the reader must maintain the group's composition to understand the text.

When considering the cohesion of texts, exophoric references are non-cohesive while pronouns falling within the 'other roles' category e.g. 'he', 'she' 'it' are cohesive because they are anaphoric or cataphoric.

Texts sometimes contain direct speech and when this occurs the exophoric reference becomes endophoric; this is a further important point, for early reading books contain more than their fair share of direct speech.

Pronouns perform fundamental roles in communication, especially in written texts, but educators often assume that learners have fully mastered them either before compulsory schooling begins or that they are small and insignificant and not worthy of instruction. Whatever the reason, little attention appears to be paid to them in school. To reinforce the point about the way pronouns refer back to their antecedents, and for a little humour, look at the effect produced when Lewis Carroll broke the anaphoric relations, by leaving out the antecedents of the pronouns in a poem from *Alice's Adventures in Wonderland*.

> They told me you had been to her,
> And mentioned me to him:
> She gave me a good character
> But said I could not swim.

He sent them word I had not gone
(We know it to be true):
If she should push the matter on,
What would become of you?

I gave her one, they gave him two,
You gave us three or more;
They all returned from him to you,
Though they were mine before.

If I or she should chance to be
Involved in this affair
He trusts to you to set them free
Exactly as we were.

My notion was that you had been
(Before she had this fit)
An obstacle that came between
Him, and ourselves, and it.

Don't let him know she likes them best,
For this must even be
A secret, kept from all the rest,
Between yourself and me.

Here we do not know who 'they', 'me', 'you', 'her', etc. are, and we are left with a feeling of vagueness from only having half the meaning of the poem, since pronouns separated from their antecedents leave us searching for meaning. It may be that slow readers experience a similar vagueness when they are unable to span the distance between the two ends of a cohesive tie.

Acquisition of the personal reference system

Think for a moment of young children acquiring their mother tongue. They have first to distinguish themselves from others, establish an identity of their own before they can appreciate the first person pronouns, 'I', 'me', 'my', and 'mine'. The child has to learn that when he is the speaker in a conversation he refers to himself as 'I', but will also come to realise that when the person he has been addressing as 'you' is speaking, then that person becomes 'I' in the conversation and he becomes the 'you'. The first person pronoun is not fixed. 'I' does not always refer to 'me' in conversations! The usage of pronouns depends on the roles played in the communication event; how to play these roles (the conversational rules) has to be learned, as well as how to apply the pronouns to these roles. Renira Huxley at Edinburgh University observed the development of personal pronoun usage in two children from age 2 years 3 months through to four years. In her analysis Huxley (1970), related how the little boy, Douglas, used his own name, Douglas, in the early months and how the use of 'I' became dominant by 3 years 1 month. We should note here that there is considerable variation in individual language acquisition and that the girl in the study, Katriona, used the pronoun 'I' correctly from the beginning of the observations. These two children did not confuse 'I' and 'you' as has been reported by other observers. Katriona is reported to have used anaphoric personal pronouns especially 'he', 'she', correctly (i.e. as adults would) from the beginning of the observations, whereas Douglas did not do so regularly. By about 3 years 5 months Douglas used 'he' regularly to refer back to a person he had previously mentioned and the correct use of 'she' was established at more or less the same time.

Mention is made by Renira Huxley of the meaning conveyed by 'you' (plural). She suggests that 'you' can convey (1) You who are here and you who are also here, and it can mean (2) you who are here and someone else who is not present. This pronoun was used very little by the two children and its second application not at all. Katriona had no trouble with the plural pronoun 'they' after she had first used it at 2 years 8 months, but Douglas, although he used 'they' sooner than Katriona, used 'them' concurrently: 'them are only little, aren't they'. In her summary discussion Renira Huxley remarks that Katriona had no difficulty with any subject pronoun except 'I' and 'you' (this was a special case for her) but the acquisition pattern of Douglas differed. 'I' was correctly used after 3 years 3 months, then 'he', 'she', 'they' were used correctly after a period of ten weeks. Another fourteen weeks passed before 'we' was correctly used. That is, seven months passed between the correct use of 'I' and 'we'.

Renira Huxley concluded that one should be careful not to use subject pronouns as predictors of general language development in the early years as other areas of language are developing alongside and will also be making demands. Apart from the analysis summarised above, there is mention in the article of a comparison made with eight-year-old children where 'the biggest difference was in the anaphoric pronouns (which were used with greater ease and frequency by the older children; particularly in reference to a previously mentioned person) and in the pronoun addressing remarks to the other person participating in the discourse: you.'

This review of the acquisition of pronouns by very young children, albeit only two of them, gives us some indication of the way in which pronoun usage develops but, as with other aspects of language development, we should beware of jumping to conclusions. The reference to some older children is, of course, of particular interst for our purposes, and we now go on to look at ways in which older children learn to distinguish between pronouns in simple word recognition situations.

Later development of personal reference

In some research carried out by the author (Chapman, 1975), the development of children's understanding of pronouns was further explored. The children were aged five to eleven years and the information was collected in ordinary classroom settings. If you refer back to Table 1 p.00, you will find that the set of English pronouns were arranged there in terms of their function during communication. The table showed that some pronouns were singular, others plural; some were applied by the speaker to himself while others referred to the addressee. Others varied according to gender, and so on. Children learn to use these pronouns as they acquire their natural language, but such are the intricacies involved that often, when extra demands are made, especially during early reading, their knowledge might be found to be insecure.

Working within the global framework of the cohesion model that has been introduced, an investigation was subsequently made into the way primary school children coped with pronouns in texts. It was decided to look at the reading ability of two classes containing some 74 eight-year-old children (Chapman, 1979a). This particular age-group was chosen because it was thought that most of the children would be proficient at word recognition and fluent in reading a simple story. It was hoped that the investigation would shed some light on the situation where a child is moving from the beginning reading stage to that of the developing reading stage, that is, from the time he or she is stumbling from word to word to the time when fluency is clearly demonstrated by phrasing and flow when reading aloud. It was hypothesised that part of this fluency would result from the ability to recognise the semantic unity of a text by correctly identifying anaphoric and other cohesive ties.

The 74 children chosen for the research attended a First School in a new town. The population served by the school is a mixture of socio-economic groupings. The Head Teacher reported that the full range of ability was represented in the school and that no children taking part were either physically or mentally handicapped. The average age of the children was 8½ years. The class teachers were asked to arrange the children into two groups: those they would class as being fluent and those non-fluent. These teacher judgements of their pupils' capabilities were supplemented by the results of a graded word reading test. As often happens, the teacher ratings were found to agree very substantially with the reading test.

It was decided to construct some materials specially for the testing so as to study systematically the children's performance with pronouns. Seven stories were especially written for the research to the following specifications. Firstly, to maintain motivation and to provide adequate context, all seven texts were in a style closely resembling the narratives found in ordinary school primers. Secondly, the target pronouns that were being investigated were incorporated into the text in such a way as to interfere as little as possible with the flow of the story. Thirdly, the position of the pronouns in the text was varied so that positional effects within sentences and paragraphs were reduced as much as was feasible. This was to ensure that a pronoun did not always fall, for example, at the beginning of a sentence. Fourthly, so as to cover the full range of pronouns, a grammatical model provided by Gleason (1969) was followed. The stories were arranged to test the target pronouns thus:

Story 1	I, me, my, mine
Story 2	our, ours, us, we
Story 3	his, him, he
Story 4	yours, your, you
Story 5	them, their, theirs, they
Story 6	she, hers, her
Story 7	its, it

Fifthly, a deletion procedure was employed and the target pronouns were deleted systematically at intervals of approximately every seventh word. So as to give the readers some context, every story has a run-in paragraph of three to four sentences. Each story was printed on a separate sheet and the seven were put together to make a small individual booklet.

The completion tasks demanded more of the children than a straightforward reading task where the word is actually present on the page, awaiting recognition. From reading the context provided, the child had to select the correct pronoun from his or her memory store to fit the sense of the passage, and then write it in the space. He or she had, in other words, to supply the appropriate cohesive link word.

It was thought that this might be a difficult task for some of the younger children in the group, so half the booklets had the pronouns that had been deleted printed in a list at the bottom of the page. Their order was jumbled so that a definite act of selection had to be made. It was hoped that this would prevent the children just copying the pronouns willy-nilly into the spaces. The two original groups, that is one containing fluent and the other non-fluent readers were subdivided so that half of each group would have the words provided and half not.

Here is an example from the experimental material. Story 5, after the introductory paragraph, went like this:

> One day some boys went fishing in the river with fishing nets and jam jars. The fishes were playing tag among the waterweeds and so_____ did not see the net. One by one _____ were caught. The boys took _____ home in a jam jar. (See full story in Appendix 2.)

In inserting the correct pronoun, the reader has to select the word which will, in normal reading, signal the cohesive element.

The results of this work showed, as was expected, that fluent readers could supply most of the missing pronouns whereas the non-fluent readers were less able to do so. Furthermore, even when the missing pronouns were supplied, although there was a general improvement in the performance. the non-fluent readers improved very little. The findings of the research work (Chapman, 1979b) gave support to the proposition that the children's ability to perceive the cohesive ties during reading could well be a major factor in reading fluency and hence in reading development. It may be that the language development of the children in the non-fluent group had not reached a sufficient level of maturity to cope with filling in the gaps, but more of this later.

To sum up, we noted that the development of the underlying

knowledge of the organisation of the set of pronouns in English does not reach that of an adult until some children are, at least, of middle school age. Moreover, when the language development aspect was applied to the reading situation it was found that only those eight-year-olds that were judged as fluent by their teachers could really cope with the task involved.

It is suggested that these findings demonstrate that one of the sections of the reference group of cohesive ties, that of personal reference, or pronouns which have definite anaphoric relationships, is more clearly associated with fluent reading than may have been appreciated. It was felt to be important to follow some of these early, and as yet, very tentative research findings to see at what age children began to display the proficiency that the author had at first expected at the younger age. Another investigation was planned, therefore, to extend the work (Chapman and Stokes, 1980). To achieve the aims of the investigation the number of specially written stories was doubled, the age-range extended to older children and the number of children enlarged. The same procedure was adopted as before and pronouns were deleted in the same fashion as previously and the fourteen texts assembled in random order into individual booklets.

As well as the eight-year-old age group, further groups aged eleven and fourteen years were chosen and the numbers in each group raised to ninety per group. The total number of children involved in the work was now 270 and this number was judged to be large enough to give more representative results. The children in the eight-year-old group attended two First Schools in the same small town, one in the centre and one built to serve a new housing estate. Those in the eleven-year-old age group attended a Middle School and those in the fourteen-year-old group attended an Upper School. The Middle School is in a neighbouring, more industrial area. It has a four-class entry with mixed-ability class teaching. The Upper School is situated in the same area and serves the families of both the town and outlying villages. The school is a large one taking children at twelve years, with 350 children in each year plus a large sixth form. The children are allocated, following tests, to three ability-bands on entry. Four classes spanning the full range of ability took part in the research.

All the testing was carried out by the same person with the help and co-operation of the class teachers involved. The First School children were allowed 45 minutes to complete the fourteen stories. However, to prevent fatigue, a break for play-time was arranged half way through the testing. The Middle and Upper School children had the same timing without the break.

If all the pronouns were replaced correctly the maximum score for the fourteen stories was 108. The average scores for the groups are shown in the graph in Figure 8.

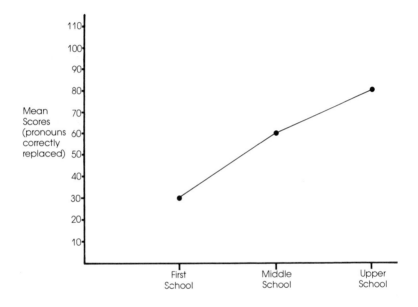

Figure 8. Graph of average scores on the fourteen stories with deleted pronouns for the First, Middle and Upper School

Predictably, the average scores increased with age. The Middle School children's average score was double that of the First School children, but the Upper School's results did not reach as high a score as was expected. In fact only one child from the ninety in the fourteen-year-old group achieved the maximum score.

These findings were of concern to the researchers, especially when the results of the fourteen-year-olds were not much nearer the maximum score possible than those of the eleven-year-olds. After all, the task was only to replace pronouns in simple story texts.

However, although various alterations were made to the texts and to the conditions, in order to make sure there was nothing that presented the children with problems of which we were unaware, the overall results remained the same.

From these results and others that will be discussed later, there are clear indications that the ability of children to replace simple pronouns is still developing in the Upper School. It is, therefore, at least one small area of reading that needs attention in all schools. It may well be that in our efforts to attend to other areas of curriculum we have neglected some of the skills that are at the very root of our ability to both understand and construct texts. What is more, there are clear indications from some classroom trials that the position can be improved quickly through efficient teaching.

These investigations have shown that children's linguistic awareness of personal reference is still developing within the secondary school. Personal reference is only one of the three which make up the reference group of cohesive ties. The others within this group are demonstrative and comparative reference.

Demonstrative reference

Halliday and Hasan explain demonstrative reference as 'a form of verbal pointing'. This, like the notion of cohesive ties itself, provides a useful analogy for teaching purposes. The functioning of the demonstrative group of ties helps the speaker or author to make reference by way of locating an object or process in space or time.

As in the case of pronouns, we find indications in early language acquisition research of potential problems that might arise when demands are put on children's language development by the curriculum in schools.

An important point to remember with this sub-group of reference ties, is the location of the point from which reference is made during communication. Whether it is in speech, or when conversation is written down in texts, the speaker or author has to make the situation explicit by giving demonstrative reference cues. In all these there is need for the point of reference to be stated so that other people and things can be located in space.

Take for instance the two demonstratives *here* and *there*. These are arranged in Table 2 according to proximity. But *near* or *far*, from whom or what? In order to comprehend these two cohesive ties, it is necessary to take the speaker as the reference point and because

Table 2 Reference cohesive ties: demonstrative

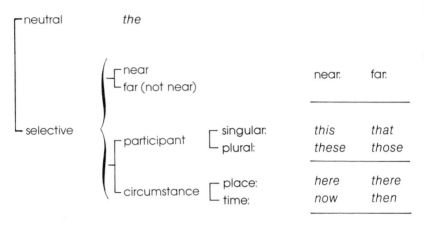

(From Halliday and Hasan 1976, p.57)

children are known to experience difficulty in their early years in taking another viewpoint, we might expect problems to occur. Some children may confuse or be unable to identify the location of the point of reference. This is especially true of those whose language ability appears low on entering school, and things often become worse for those same children later in schooling as the pressure to master formal, academic registers increases. Doubtless in all these particular details it follows that those who are learning English as a second or foreign language in our schools will need to have these features made explicit.

In some experimental work Charney (1979) traced the comprehension of words like 'here' and 'there' in children aged 2 years 6 months to 3 years 6 months. Contrary to what was expected, the children did not comprehend the words with self as a reference point first. 'Instead' the words appear to be understood first with respect to an inconsistent reference point before children learn that the reference point is always the speaker.' As we saw with the pronouns, 'I' is related to the speaker and is not always 'me', similarly with 'here' and 'there', for 'here' to the speaker is 'there' to the listener and so on. The point of reference is constantly moving and can cause confusion for some children; and for some this early confusion continues well into later schooling. In studies of older children by Webb and Abrahamson (1976) and Clark and Sengul (1978), situations where the child shared the speaker's perspective were contrasted with one that did not. Webb and Abrahamson found their children were still having some difficulty with 'this' and 'that' by age seven years. Clark and Sengul, testing 'here', 'there', 'this' and 'that', found that 'here' and 'there' were not mastered until around age four and 'this' and 'that' not until shortly afterwards.

Using our previous work as a guide, we probed children's underlying language ability using the gap technique. In some unpublished pilot research undertaken at the Open University, children between the ages of eleven and twelve years were given some stories where these demonstratives had been deleted. They were required to replace them in the same way as was done with the pronouns reported earlier. In the stories there were twenty-seven deletions, three of each of the demonstratives as set out in Table 2 i.e. 'the', 'this', 'that', 'these', 'those', 'here', 'there', 'now' and 'then'. The scores of the forty-two children (twenty boys and twenty-two girls) ranged from 0-20 (max. 27) with a mean of 12.0. In other words, on a simple completion task which concentrated on these cohesive features, the results of the class were below the 50 per cent level.

All the results of the research into cohesive ties so far carried out have had a similar pattern; on simple gap exercises the results have been much lower than expected. In the comparative section that is to follow, and even more so with the large group of conjunctions (pp. 139–40), for example, the results are the same. They are poor in the opinion of not only the researchers but also the teachers in the many schools who have been kind enough to help us in our work. Why then is this so?

As remarked earlier, the answer must partly lie in teachers' traditional reliance on pupils' implicit language knowledge, and resultant failure to give explicit instruction in those areas of language which we are concerned with here. The outlook, however, is encouraging, for when relevant findings of linguistic and other disciplines are applied to the study of the reading process, teachers are supplied with many new insights that yield pedagogical possibilities. For example, we are now able to speculate much more clearly what it is that creates the cohesion of a passage, what are the actual words and phrases that help it to 'hang together'. It is likely that cohesion is a major factor in the readability and thereby comprehension of texts.

But to return to the demonstratives and their functioning as cohesive ties, the important ones – 'this', 'these', 'that', and 'those' – are often found in anaphoric relations, giving us the potential for indicating proximity. The singular and plural, 'these' and 'those', are similarly available. Look at the cohesive ties in this simple passage for instance.

The Dog and the Meat

There was once a dog who had stolen a piece of meat from a butcher's shop. As (he) was crossing a river with ⌐this⌐ piece of meat in (his) mouth, (he) saw (his) reflection in the water. Mistaking (his) reflection for another dog with another piece of meat, (he) thought (he) would try to get hold of ⌐that⌐ piece of meat, too. But, in trying to wrench the piece of meat from ⌐the⌐ mouth of the other dog, (he) dropped the meat (he) already had.

(From *Twenty Famous Fables,* adapted and told by Ann Webb (1974) Nelson and Sons Ltd.)
Key: ○ personal reference
        □ demonstrative reference

We have already noticed the personal pronoun cohesive ties, and in this short passage 'he' is used six times and 'his' thrice, referring back to the dog. Now look at the function of the words this and that; this points to the piece of meat mentioned in the previous sentence and that to the piece reflected in the water. One is 'near', if you like, the other 'far', although it is in fact a reflection.

You will notice in Table 2 that Halliday and Hasan classify 'this' and 'that' as near and far indicators, similarly with the plurals these, and those. You will find that 'that' in extended texts is nearly always anaphoric and that 'this' can be both anaphoric and cataphoric. Notice also 'the' in the passage 'from the mouth'. Here the definite article 'the' is thought of as a non-selective determinant, specifying something so that it can be identified. In the case above it specifies the mouth of the other dog. The word 'the' has no content of its own and can only indicate that the item is identifiable and thus, according to Halliday and Hasan, 'the' resembles the demonstratives.

Comparative reference

As with demonstrative reference, Halliday and Hasan supply a systematic table of comparative reference.

Table 3   Reference cohesive ties: comparative

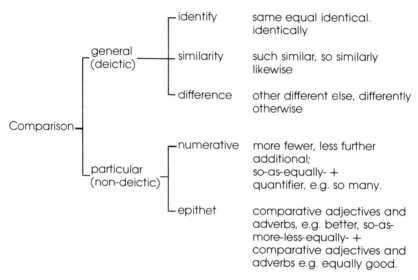

(From Halliday and Hasan, 1976.p.76)

In this, comparison is analysed into general and particular. General comparative reference is further sub-divided into identity, similarity, and difference. General comparison is to do with likeness, whether the object or thing is the same or identical, similar, or different. Again, as with personal and demonstrative reference, the comparison may reside in the situation or within the text – it can be exophoric or endophoric. Again, when endophoric, the relationship can be either anaphoric or cataphoric. The implications for the teachers' scrutiny of these comparative features are particularly strong when children are reading, for example, present-day mathematics texts. If children can be given a clear understanding of the relationships indicated by the comparative cohesive ties some of their problems with the mathematics might be avoided.

Particular comparison in this part of the reference system is concerned with the quantity or quality of the property being referred to in the text. For example, one interesting facet that may account for some of the problems of reading is the pluri-functional nature of some of the words we are calling cohesive ties. In an interesting article, Karmiloff-Smith (1977) traces the way in which the usage of 'the same' develops. Young children at first use 'the same' to cover both functions 'same one' and 'same kind'. It is her view that the youngest children in her studies generally understand one expression for several functions. This finding could be extended to our present topic for if, later in reading, similar kinds of words have pluri-functions e.g. 'do', 'one', 'some', then teachers might check that when they are cohesive, their linkage function is appreciated.

Summary

In this chapter we have seen that some linguists are now beginning to look beyond the boundary of the sentence to those features that create texts. Among the many linguistic mechanisms involved is that of anaphora, the process of linking what is being read now with what went before.

It was shown that children learn many of these language features implicitly and that sorting out the plurality of uses may be subject to a lengthy developmental process which continues throughout the years of compulsory schooling.

It was also noted that communication through texts relied on the function of two facets: linguistic knowledge or awareness, and prior or world knowledge.

The reference system of cohesive ties was seen to be most important, a fundamental part of the semantic, or meaning, system of language. It was also shown, using the pronoun system as an example, that children's first acquisition continued in later reading development. The chapter ended with a brief examination of the other two sets of reference cohesive ties, those of demonstrative and comparative reference.

5 The cohesive effects of substitution and ellipsis

Meaning and context

In previous chapters I drew attention to the fact that when we are speaking to each other, many of the words we use to convey our messages rely on the context of the situation for the avoidance of ambiguity. That is, they are not ambiguous to speakers and hearers since they can interpret the meaning directly from the situation in which messages are being exchanged. You will recall the point made earlier that, in conversation, apart from on the telephone, you are physically present in the situation. You will know to a greater or lesser extent the person to whom you are speaking and also the characteristics of the place where you are, as well as numerous other obvious details. In speech, then, we regard the situational context as an integral part of the communication, and as hearers, we can understand some of the meaning of the words used by the person speaking to us only by our awareness of the situational context and other non-verbal factors. This process, in turn, is anticipated by the speaker, who leaves certain things unsaid because the situation is perfectly obvious to speaker and audience alike.

This basic point about meaning and its relationship with situational context has been emphasised because some of its features are absent in the written text. This must be so; since the reader is not actually present in the situation being written about in the text and, therefore, needs extra cues or needs the implicit made explicit. From these cues inferences may be made as to the author's intended meaning. The author has to recreate, or build up, the situation in the text so that references can be identified from within the text. Much depends on authors, who may at times provide insufficient contextualisation for unimpeded comprehension.

We shall continue in this chapter to spell out more of the linguistic features that go to assist the creation of texts and in particular cohesion, that property of text that provides linkages for the reader and is important during the comprehending process.

Substitution

We have seen how personal, demonstrative and comparative elements make reference to other parts of the text anaphorically or cataphorically so that meanings can be integrated. In this section we look at another group of small words, the substitutes, which behave in much the same way as reference, but linking words or clauses. Halliday and Hasan (1976) give the following list of substitutes:

> nominal: one, ones, same
> verbal: do
> clausal: so, not

Substitution by 'one'

Remembering how pronouns work, read this short extract and in particular notice the use of the word 'one':

> Making toffee wasn't at all the easy thing the article in the magazine made it out to be and it was all most disappointing, particularly as it was the first time he'd tried his paw at making sweets.
>
> The magazine in question was an old one of Mrs. Brown's and he had first come across it earlier in the day when he'd been at a bit of a loose end. Normally Paddington didn't think much of Mrs Brown's magazines. They were much too full of advertisements and items about how to keep clean and look smart for his liking, but this one had caught his eye because it was a special cookery number.
>
> (From *Paddington at Large* by Michael Bond (1962) Puffin (1966), Penguin Books. My italics.)

In this extract the first 'one' refers back to 'magazine' and stands instead of the word 'magazine', but as it occurs within a sentence does not add much to the cohesion of the passage. The second 'one' which is modified by 'this' does add to cohesion. In this instance, 'one' refers back to 'they' which in turn refers back to 'magazines' at the end of the previous sentence. The word 'one' used in this way is said to be a substitute for the actual word and substitutes are cohesive.

Look at a further example in the following passage:

> My school was in the nearest village, two miles away. We didn't have a car of our own. We could afford one, but the walk took only half an hour and I didn't mind that in the least.
>
> (From *Danny, Champion of the World* by Roald Dahl (1975) Puffin (1977), Penguin Books. My italics.)

Now contrast the two 'ones' in this passage:

> Well, it would do me no good to run away. There were other bears in the woods. I might meet one at any time. I might as well deal with this one as with another.
>
> (From *Little House in the Big Woods* by Laura Ingalls Wilder (1932) Puffin (1963), Penguin Books. My italics.)

Clearly in this piece of text 'one', like the pronouns we examine in Chapter 4, refers anaphorically to 'the bears' mentioned in the previous sentence. In the passage the first 'one' refers to any one of several bears and the second, modified by the demonstrative 'this', a cohesive tie of proximity, refers to the particular bear confronting the storyteller. Notice below, how the second 'one' can be replaced by the word 'bear'; the process being reversible, but in the first the indefinite article has to be introduced.

> I might meet a bear at any time. I might as well deal with this bear as with another.

We have seen that 'one' can be a substitute indicating to the reader that he must seek the identity of 'one' elsewhere in the text. In this way we can think of the substitute 'one' acting as a counter filling a slot which might have been occupied by the actual word or words previously used. In this case the second 'one' is a substitute for 'bear', but the first is associated with a special type of substitution called ellipsis. Thus 'one' functions on both occasions anaphorically across sentences: it contributes to the cohesion of the passage. We will look in more detail at ellipsis later in the chapter.

In nominal positions like those above, we get 'one', 'ones', and 'same' as substitutes. Before looking at examples of these, we should note that 'one', 'ones', and 'same' may occur in other positions, some of which may not be substitutions and are thereby not cohesive. 'One' can be a personal pronoun – or a numeral – and not be cohesive; it can be a general noun, a thing, person, or creature, and not be a cohesive tie. Care needs to be taken, therefore, when we are analysing texts for cohesive ties to make sure the word (or words) in question is a substitute. Table 4 below gives the forms of 'one' and related items.

Table 4. The forms of 'one', and related items

Item	Class	Function	Phonological status
1 one, ones	nominal substitute	Head (always modified)	salient or weak
2 one (they, you, we)	personal pronoun	Head (never modified)	weak
3 one (two, three . . .)	cardinal numeral	Numerative; Modifier or Head	salient
4 one, some (both, other)	cardinal numeral	Deictic; Modifier or Head	salient
5 a/an, some (any)	determiner ('indefinite article')	Deictic; Modifier	reduced
6 one/some (any)	determiner ('indefinite article')	Deictic; Head (never modified	weak
7 one, ones (thing)	pronoun	Head	salient
8 thing, person, creature, etc	general noun	Head (usually with the)	weak (when anaphoric

(After Halliday and Hasan, 1976)

Substitution by 'same'

The word *same*, often accompanied by 'the', functions as a nominal substitute. Sometimes *the same* stands instead of an entire nominal group, as Halliday and Hasan point out with the following illustration:

A   I'll have two poached eggs on toast, please.

B   I'll have *the same*.

Here 'the same' substitutes for 'two poached eggs on toast' and incidentally, can be distinguished from 'the same' as in 'the same eggs' which would be reference, not substitution, implying the actual eggs . .

You will find many other occurrences of 'same' and 'the same' as substitutions. e.g. 'say the same', 'be the same', 'do the same', etc. Compare these usages in the following examples:

'What's the matter?' she asked. 'Leave me be,' he replied. 'I'm sulking!'

'But people don't say when they are sulking; they just sulk,' objected Susan.

'I'm not people. I'm one scarecrow. You've asked and I've told you,' snapped Gummidge.

'Sometimes I sulks for hours and sometimes I sulks for weeks; it's in the family, we're all *the same*.'

(From *Worzel Gummidge* by B.E.Todd, Puffin (1941), Penguin Books. My italics)

So Sam sang again in a thin high voice, but he changed the words, he was in such a fright.

'Dear Mister Fox,
He needs a Christmas box,
A coat and a hat
And a pair of yellow socks.' murmured Sam.
'It doesn't sound quite *the same* to me,' said the fox . . .

(From *Magic in My Pocket. A Selection of Tales* by Alison Utley (1957), Penguin Books. My italics)

If you inspect the use of 'the same' in the first and second extracts:

. . . We're all *the same* and

. . . quite *the same*,

you find that *the same* acts as a substitute standing for something that has occurred before (i.e. 'sulks' and 'sang').

You may have noted 'one' in the first of these two pieces of text. Here, however, it is a number modifying the noun 'scarecrow' and so is not a substitute. You cannot replace this 'one' by 'scarecrow' as we did with 'bear' for 'one' earlier.

Substitution by 'do'

The word 'do', which has other usages as does 'one', occurs as a verbal substitute; that is, it frequently substitutes for the verb and other elements. (It belongs to the lexical scatter, *does, did, doing, done*.) The *done* in the passage below is given by Halliday and Hasan as an example of verbal substitution:

He never really succeeded in his ambitions. He might have *done*, one felt, had it not been for the restlessness of his nature.

You will remember how the process of anaphora, by making reference across the sentence boundary, adds to cohesion: here 'done' acts in the same way and is a verbal substitute for 'succeeded in his ambitions'.

Now compare 'did' in the following passage:

> Well, you know, Miss Golightly, you took the compact I'd got for Mummy's birthday present, and I did so want to give it to her today and I asked William to get it for me and he didn't, but Herbert *did*. He went right into your study this afternoon and took it out of your drawer, and I suppose he took the wrong one.
>
> (From *William and the Tramp* by Richmal Crompton, George Newnes Ltd. My italics.)

Here 'did' substitutes for 'got it for me', that is, 'He didn't, but Herbert got it for me'.

It is sometimes tricky to sort out which function 'do' is performing, but if you remember that 'do' can be replaced by the actual words you will be able to distinguish between the functions. Notice the preceding 'didn't' which is elliptical and, as we shall see, is also a type of substitution and is cohesive. Here we understand the words 'get it for me', i.e. 'he didn't get it for me'.

Substitution by 'so' and 'not'

We have looked briefly at examples of nominal and verbal substitutions; the other type is clausal substitution which involves the words 'so' and 'not'. Here, as the terminology suggests, it is not a word or words, but a clause that is substituted by 'so' or 'not'. The following extracts are chosen to illustrate the use of *so* as a clausal substitute.

> He spoke softly and his eyes were sombre as he looked at Ged. 'You thought, as a boy, that a mage is one who can do anything. *So* I thought, once. *So* did we all. And the truth is that as a man's real power grows and his knowledge widens, ever the way he can follow grows narrower: until at last he chooses nothing, but does only and wholly what he must do . . .'
>
> (From *A Wizard of Earthsea* by Ursula Le Guin, Puffin (1968), Penguin Books. My italics.)

In this extract 'so' substitutes for the clause, 'a mage is one who can do anything', in both instances.

In most texts 'so' occupies a final position, but in these examples it takes up the initial position. We find the same usage in expressions like 'so he said, 'so I believe', etc. 'So' is cohesive and in this case anaphoric. Halliday and Hasan give the following as an example of the negative form:

Has everyone gone home? I hope *not*.

Here 'not' is a substitute for 'that everyone has not gone home'. Another example where 'not so' occurs as a substitute is shown in the following extract:

> The workers were discontented. One day when both the Marquis and the Marchioness were away a mob attacked the castle, sacked it and set fire to it. The dogs and horses belonging to the estate were rescued by the workers themselves. But *not so* poor Pippenella. In her silver cage hung outside the tower window, hundreds of feet above the ground, she was overlooked and left on the wall of the blazing building . . .
>
> (From *Dr. Dolittle's Caravan* by Hugh Lofting (1927), Puffin (1968), Penguin Books. My italics.)

Here 'not so' substitutes anaphorically for 'was not rescued by the workers'.

Substitution, then, includes the words 'one', 'ones', and 'same', in nominal groups; 'do', in verbal groups; and 'so', 'not', and 'not so' in clausal groups.

The development of pluri-functional terms

You might have been struck by the fact that these words, as with pronouns, are some of the most frequently used in English. We might pause here to reflect on this, for as we have pointed out previously we can often be misled by children's performance in oral reading into thinking that because children are able to read a passage aloud they can also fully comprehend it. Furthermore, because a word appears to be actively present in a child's vocabulary in this way, we cannot assume that that child can follow its meaning in all situations. So many of the words we are discussing as cohesive elements play different roles according to their position in the structure of the text. The same word can have many uses. It is, therefore, pluri-functional.

Some work by Annette Karmiloff-Smith (1977) showed that children between two and seven years interpret 'the same' to mean the 'same kind' in contexts where it actually means 'the same one'. The instance reported concerned the slugs one of the children ('J') went to see every morning.

> At 2.7 she cried: *There it is* on seeing one, and when we saw another ten yards further on she cried: *There's the slug again*. I (Karmiloff-Smith) answered, *But isn't it another?* J went back to see the first one. *Is it the*

same? Yes. *Another slug?* Yes. *Another or the same?* The question obviously had no meaning for J.

Her experiments showed that the change of interpretation from 'same kind' to 'same as' is very significantly a function of age (i.e. development) and of extralinguistic context within each age-group. In her discussion of her experimental results, when referring to 'the logical yet ungrammatical forms' used by the children, Karmiloff-Smith points out that they 'tend to disappear once the child implicitly allows for one expression to have more than one function depending on the context of the utterances'. She notes also that 'small children seem to use language exophorically in reference to the extralinguistic context, rather than anaphorically, and this probably also affects the younger child's preferred interpretation of "same kind".' Karmiloff-Smith's discussion also includes important points about the role of language when concepts of development are being explored and how cautious we should be to avoid misinterpretations.

From these detailed investigations we have a growing store of knowledge regarding specific areas of children's linguistic development. And as time goes on, research is gradually putting together pieces of the giant jig-saw puzzle of initial acquisition and later development. As noted earlier, most of the work has been concerned with early acquisition and it will be some time before detail is available for guidance as to later development. However, within the work done, important insights like learning how to process anaphoric relations, have far-reaching implications for teachers throughout the age-range of compulsory schooling.

You could now take some of the texts you are using with your pupils and make simple analyses of some of these features, as it is important to discover at first hand how they operate. Having found the cohesive ties, you will then be able to make deletions using the procedures outlined later in Chapter 8. Remember that you can achieve a great deal by first arranging the activities of individuals followed by group discussion of the features deleted.

Ellipsis

Returning to the discussion of substitution and remembering that the words 'one', 'some', 'do', 'so' could be used as substitutes in appropriate contexts, we come now to another contributor to cohesion, which is called ellipsis. As you may recall we came across this first in the extract on page 75 where the use of the substitute 'one' was discussed.

Look at the following extract

> Nearer they came to the Edge, until it towered above them, then they turned to the right along a road which kept to the foot of the hill. On one side*[1] lay the fields, and on the other *[2] the steep slopes. (From *The Weirdstone of Brisingamen* by Alan Garner (1960), Puffin (1963), Penguin Books.)

The ellipsis in the second sentence, as indicated by the numbered asterisks, demonstrates the way in which this particular kind of substitution works. The reader, if required, will usually supply at *[1] the words 'of the road', and 'side of the road lay' at *[2]. Quirk *et al.* (1972) state:

> In a strict sense of ellipsis, words are ellipsed only if they are uniquely recoverable, ie there is no doubt as to what words are to be supplied, and it is possible to add the recovered words to the sentence.

Or again,

> Ellipsis is most commonly an abbreviating device that reduces redundancy. A major use of ellipsis is the avoidance of repetition, and in this respect it is like substitution, which can often be used instead of ellipsis.

Note the cohesive effect achieved in the example above where the word 'road', which is presupposed, lies some twelve words back. The important point about ellipsis is that the author, in choosing not to repeat himself, nonetheless cues the reader to make the reference back, and yet the words that are presupposed are *not* actually repeated. For instance, the author could have written:

> On the one side of the road lay the fields and on the other *side of the road lay* the steep slopes.

In this way the writer would have made his message transparent but this would have made the passage repetitious and inelegant. Now look at a further example:

> Andrew and Sally went to catch frogs in the pond.
> Andrew caught three* and Sally caught two*.
> Andrew put his* in the paddling pool at home but Sally let hers go.

At the three asterisked positions where ellipsis occurs it is possible to expand what was said or written by supplying the word 'frogs'. We often expand utterances to help the young or the non-native speaker understand.

Sometimes the reader has to supply single words, sometimes phrases, and sometimes clauses. Whatever the mechanics of the placing of ellipsis in the text, something is presupposed, and, as the words are not physically present, they have to be supplied by the reader, or, as it is sometimes put, 'understood'.

As with substitution, ellipsis can be verbal as well as nominal. In the following extract, only one word, a verb, is involved.

> I knew it would do no good to try to go around him. He would follow me into the dark woods, where he could see better than I could.*

(From *Little House in the Big Woods* by Laura Ingalls Wilder (1932), Puffin (1963), Penguin Books)

Here the verb 'see' is to be supplied, presupposing the previous 'see'. In this instance, the relationship is within a sentence; we are more interested in the cohesive ties across sentence boundaries.

Sometimes ellipsis involves a clause, and this, as the term implies, involves the expansion of more than one word. Some examples given by Halliday and Hasan (1976, p.200) are:

	Presupposed clause	Elliptical form	Substitute form	Full form
a)	Has the plane landed?	Yes it has	Yes it has done	Yes it has landed
b)	Keep out of sight till the plane lands	It has	It has done	It has landed
c)	Who was playing the piano?	Peter was	Peter was doing	Peter was playing the piano

These examples give us an indication of the way ellipsis and substitution function in texts.

From the above you will have noted that some of the cohesive ties fall on the borderline between categories. When analysing the texts you use in schools therefore you should note that the division into sub-categories is not watertight. Halliday and Hasan point this out saying.

> It has been emphasised already that the classification of cohesive relations into different types should not be seen as implying a rigid

division into watertight compartments. There are many instances of coheisve forms which lie on the borderline between two types and could be interpreted as one or the other. (p.88)

This is important for the practising teacher for the effective point in teaching about cohesion is the linkages that alert the reader to the flow of meaning through the passage, not the analysis into sub-categories.

Practical application

You may already have wondered how this aspect of cohesion might be tackled in the classroom. As the requirement is to expand the expression by supplying words where they are ellipsed, obviously we cannot delete words that are not physically on the page. However, the following method has been found useful. It consists simply of denying the truth that is assumed by the ellipsis. Look at the following example:

> Bill and Simon were racing for the fence. Whoever got there first would be safe from the maddened bull behind them. Bill could go no faster, but Simon could *[1] and with a final effort he leapt over *[2].

Here the ellipsis indicated by the asterisks requires the expansion by (1) 'go faster' and 'the fence' at (2). (Note how elliptical substitution in (2) refers back as far as the first sentence.) If we add a further sentence to this passage: 'It was lucky they both reached the fence at the same time', we deny that Simon could go faster.

In the example about the frogs, if we alter 'but Sally let hers go' to something like 'but Sally let her butterflies go' then the ellipsed word 'frogs' that refers back to the first sentence is contradicted.

Some teachers with whom we have worked constructed booklets of passages such as these and asked their pupils to circle any elements that are odd or do not make sense. The results of this were interesting. Some of the children could not find the contradiction, some were quite amused and could be seen smiling as they worked through the booklet but were not quite sure whether they should be amused or not, and others very quickly found the oddities and worked through the booklet with great speed.

A criticism that might be levelled at this activity is worth mentioning here. This is that this is more than is normally required for reading, for the simple problem-solving nature of the task involves the use of other cognitive skills. This is certainly so, but, as we noted earlier, what is reading, if it does not contain cognitive elements? What is more, some authorities are now claiming that learning to read *per se* is directly related to reasoning (Downing 1979).

Another practical application can be easily arranged as follows. A passage by Barbara Todd (op. cit.) serves for illustration:

> When they went into the farm kitchen, they saw that a stranger was standing by the open doorway. He was a queer little bent-up man dressed in an old velveteen coat and breeches. He was talking to Mrs Braithwaite in a thin, high voice.
>
> 'I saw your scarecrow was gone,' he said. 'And I thought mebbe as how . . .'
>
> 'The master can make another *[1] for himself as easy as not,' interrupted Mrs Braithwaite. 'We don't need to pay to have an old face carved out of a turnip.'
>
> 'There's luck in tatie bogles,' replied the old man. 'Some of them are queer and some *[2] are lucky and some are no use at all. I've been making them for fifty years, and I should know something about them. I made the one that stood in Ten-acre field about twelve months ago, when I was hedging and ditching.'

Children's appreciation of ellipses can be probed by giving a number of alternatives to put where the asterisks are. Underneath the passage two columns of words could be presented thus:

*1	*2
Which of these could you put in here?	Which of these could you put in here?
1) man	1) scarecrows
2) turnip	2) turnips
3) scarecrow	3) tatie bogles
4) woman	4) men
5) face	5) faces

Activities of this type soon spring to mind once the basic relationship of ellipsis is understood. There are many instances in texts at all levels and 'Spot the ellipsis' games can be made quite progressive and informative. It is worth including these in your work, for children will soon vie with each other in finding ellipses.

The way in which ellipsis cohesive ties are processed by the skilled reader is probably one of the most interesting, for it is a good example of the unconscious knowledge of rules the mother-tongue user of English has. It appears to operate automatically without the reader being conscious of the process. This in itself makes it quite difficult to spot examples at first, such is the implicit nature of ellipsis.

It is interesting to notice that when stories are being read to young children, the adult reader will often expand expressions that have been left out by ellipsis. This can be observed particularly when the reader believes that the context is not being understood. If you wish to observe this, follow closely the text an infant teacher or parent is reading to a child, especially if that text is above the listener's present level of understanding.

Summary

In this chapter we looked first at the important relationship between meaning and context, showing how a great deal of the meaning in speech is resolved by reference to the actual physical situation of that speech. We saw also that in the written text the author relied not only on the reader's working knowledge of such contextual relationships but on their supplementation by direct description of the context.

Secondly, the cohesive ties of substitution were seen as another set of linguistic features and the words, 'one', 'same', 'do', 'so', and 'not' were shown as indicators or substitution. We noted also that these same words can function in more than one way and were therefore examples of pluri-functionality.

The cohesive function of ellipsis, a further type of substitution, was next introduced and practical activities suggested for alerting pupils to its presence in texts.

6 Cohesion by conjunctions

Conjunctions function in a different way from the other types of cohesion so far discussed. We give them, therefore, a short chapter to themselves, not only to indicate this difference but to emphasise the importance of conjunctions, or connectives, as they are sometimes called.

Their difference from the other cohesive ties lies mainly in the fact that they do not function anaphorically. Conjunctions have specific meanings and perform their connective function by presupposing the presence of other related elements in the text. They are used to make meanings in the text explicit and function mainly between pairs of sentences.

Reading and pluri-functional words

The monosyllabic words 'and', 'yet', 'so', and 'then' are given as typical instances of each of the four conjunction types. It is clear that these words are among the more easily read words and are often to be found in early word lists such as are used in word recognition tests yet, as we shall see, these same small words carry a heavy cueing function for the reader. Furthermore, they are plurifunctional. And here it is necessary to emphasise the importance of what has been pointed out before: so often, having taught children to recognise words, we tend not to teach the vastly more important relationships of which such words are a part. It is usual for children to be said to be reading when they can call out, or sound, the words on a page, and we tend to assess them by this, yet this is not reading. It is the part these frequently used words play that is so important in the comprehending process. We need, therefore, to have some method of checking that children are distinguishing between the different uses made of the same word as they re-create the meaning of texts.

The four types of conjunctions

Halliday and Hasan provide a useful summary table of conjunctions (see Appendix 3) and in this table you will find the conjunctions listed by type according to the semantic function they perform. There are four basic types known as the additive, (the 'and' type); the adversative (the 'yet' type); the temporal (the 'then' type); and the causal (the 'so' type). When reading, conjunctions confirm that the sentence that has just been read is to be connected with the following sentence and that it is the meanings that are to be integrated. Note that it is not only connection but also a confirmation of the meaning of the message. The conjunctions noted under the 'and' type, for instance, indicate the simple addition of, or an alternative to, something that has already been stated; the 'yet' type signals a comparison or contrast; the 'so' type gives the reader confirmation that one sentence is related in a causal way to the next; and the 'then' type indicates a temporal or sequential linkage. These are fundamental meaning elements and of paramount importance for comprehending, as they indicate to the reader the type of meaning relation intended by the author. In this way conjunctions create textual cohesion by directly linking sentences.

Sentence boundaries

We have said that conjunctions are found between pairs of sentences and when you try to analyse the whereabouts of the conjunctions in the texts you present to your learner readers, you may find the definition of the boundary of a sentence a problem. A sentence in spoken English is defined by Halliday and Hasan thus: 'A new sentence starts whenever there is no structural connection with what has gone before.' However, as they point out, written language has different conventions.

So we may find conjunctions in the middle of many written 'sentences'. Look at the following example which shows the cueing of the alternative by the additive, 'or':

> Water is a liquid. It can be clean enough to drink or it can be full of mud and dirt.

This could have been written in three sentences as below:

> Water is a liquid. It can be clean enough to drink. Or, it can be full of mud and dirt.
> (From *Reading 360 Readers*, Ginn and Co.,)

In written texts like this, sentence boundaries can be almost arbitrarily positioned. However, we need to be careful when considering the property of cohesion that the word, or words, under scrutiny are contributing to cohesion, for we have to recall, as we did earlier on page 79 the pluri-functional nature of some of the words under review; in some instances their function, while still important in the structure of the sentence, may not be cohesive.

Multi-word conjunctions

Some conjunctions consist of more than one word (see Appendix 4). Look at the way a time sequence is conveyed by the temporal conjunctions 'at first', 'then', 'at last' in the following pieces of text.

> The Swallow slipped slowly out towards the mouth of the bay. She made *at first* no noise and hardly any wake. *Then,* as she came clear of the northerly side of the bay, she found a little more wind, and the cheerful lapping noise began under her forefoot.

Later on the same page we read:

> *At last* John let out the main sheet.
> (From *Swallows and Amazons* by Arthur Ransome (1930), Puffin (1962), Penguin Books. My italics.)

It is evident that these multi-word conjunctions are read by the fluent reader as one unit. We will call them 'n-word conjunctions' ('n' standing for 'number') to prevent the potential confusion of the terms pluri-functional and multi-word.

In passing, we might observe that in developing children's reading skill, we need to achieve a level of proficiency at which an n-word conjunction is perceived not as separate words, but as one item. The single unit 'at the same time' is perceived as a signal cueing a fluent reader to make a particular type of semantic linkage. Consider how the beginning reader reads each word individually, and then as fluency develops the word groups are gradually perceived as one unit. Some children may not realise the signalling potential of both single words and groups of words until this is pointed out to them.

Examples of conjunctions

The following texts, chosen more or less at random from texts found in schools, illustrate (a) the four types of conjunction and (b) some n-word conjunctions.

The simple additive type of conjunction as the name implies, adds what is to follow in the text to what has already been read. For example, in the following 'And' is a simple additive conjunction:

> Old Moleskins continued to blink at her. 'Well,' he said, be off then now. *And* be back before sunset.'
>
> Griselda herself was a good housewife, but in all her days she had never seen the kitchen look like this. It was as fresh as a daisy. *And* Griselda began to sing to keep the kettle company.
>
> (From *Selected Stories and Verses* by Walter de la Mare (1952), Penguin Books. My italics.)

The next two examples are of adversative conjunctions:

Adversative (1) e.g. nevertheless

> . . . Not that he was having to pretend he felt tired for in fact it was only the cocoa steam that was keeping his eyelids open at all. *Nevertheless,* there was something about the way his whiskers were poking out on either side of the mug that suggested Mrs Bird had hit the nail on the head . . .
>
> (From *Paddington at Large* by Michael Bond op. cit.)

Adversative (2) e.g. on the other hand

> . . . the two females were very similar in behaviour, earnest, rather preoccupied, over anxious, and fussy. The two males, *on the other hand,* displayed totally different character.
>
> (From *My Family and Other Animals* by Gerald Durrell (1956) Granada.)

The latter of these two illustrations of the adversative conjunction, shows clearly how comparison is confirmed, that conjunctions sometimes consist of a number of words (n-words) and may not always be placed first in the sentence in written texts.

The following extract shows both the function of temporal single and n-word conjunctions.

Temporal e.g. 'then', 'by this time'

> Roger gave an experimental yap; then, seeing I still took no notice, he followed it up with a volley of deep, rich barks that echoed among the olives. I let him bark for about five minutes. *By this time* I felt sure Yani must be aware of our arrival. *Then* I threw the stone for Roger, and as he fled after it joyfully, I made my way round to the front of the house.
>
> (From *My Family and Other Animals* by Gerald Durrell, op.cit)

If you examine the occurrence of the temporal conjunction the first 'then' is an indication of sequence. Here is another instance where the semi-colon could be replaced by a full stop and a second sentence began by 'then' as is the case further down the passage. The n-word conjunction, *by this time*, is akin to the examples in the final column of Table 5 in Appendix 4 'Here and Now'. Notice the equivalent with 'at this point'.

Causal (1) e.g. 'otherwise'

> All the same, after Mrs Bird had spoken to him he took Paddington on one side and they had a long chat together while he explained how dangerous it was to take the back off a television receiver if you didn't know what you were doing.
>
> 'It's a good job bear's paws are well insulated, Mr Brown, ' he said as he bade goodbye to Paddington. '*Otherwise* you might not be here to tell the tale.'
>
> (From *Paddington at Large* by Michael Bond, op.cit.)

Causal (2) e.g. 'for this reason'

> 'There is the danger,' said Fenodyree. 'They mingle with others unnoticed, and can be detected only by certain marks, and that not always. *For this reason* must we shun all contact with men: the lonely places are dangerous, but to be surrounded by a crowd would be a greater risk.'
>
> (From *The Weirdstone of Brisingamen* by Alan Garner, op.cit.)

Understanding conjunctions

In some research pertinent to this topic, Katz and Brent (1968) examined the differences in children's understanding of conjunctions (they call them connectives) at three different levels: (1) correct usage in spontaneous speech, (2) selection of appropriate usage in a paired-sentence test, and (3) the ability to explain the function of connectives. The researchers wished to know what differences there were between the ability of children in (American) Grade I (i.e. about six years of age) and those in Grade VI (i.e. about twelve years of age). The most important difference between the age-groups was at level (3), the younger children being unable to explain the function of conjunctions.

Katz and Brent also found that 'the adversative connectives *but* and *although* presented far greater problems of mastery than the causal connective *because*'. Furthermore they noticed the developmental preference 'for linking causal clauses by means of causal as opposed to temporal connectives, and a preference for ordering causal clauses in a way which corresponds to the actual perceptual order of events'.

Flores d'Arcais (1980) reported a series of experiments dealing with children's knowledge of some simple relational terms in Dutch and Italian, mainly the common conjunctions. On the basis of his results it was argued that 'different strata of semantic competence exist, and that access to some levels of this knowledge emerges earlier than others'. Professor d'Arcais quotes Vygotsky (1962, p.46) in this respect when he observed that, 'the child may operate with subordinate clauses with words like because, if, when, and but, long before he grasps causal, conditional or temporal relations themselves'.

These findings, as with the other research reports given in earlier chapters, indicate potential teaching points regarding comprehending by checking specific cohesive links, like conjunctions, through texts. To do this, as I suggest later in Chapter 8, the gap technique is probably the most apposite. Here one end of a cohesive tie is deleted and the reader asked to replace it. To do this successfully the reader has to read and understand the interposing text between the two ends of the tie in order to fill in the missing word. This productive element is important on two accounts. Firstly, it can often detect when full understanding of the relationship is not present and, secondly, it meets one other major educational concern of the teacher, namely that of teaching pupils to write cohesively.

You should now be in a position to begin to analyse the texts you select for children to read, not only to observe these linguistic features yourself, but to know what to look for when teaching reading. The introduction I have given is at an elementary level only and if you wish to check what you are doing and find out more of the detail involved, you would be well advised, as I indicated at the outset, to have a copy of Halliday and Hasan's *Cohesion in English* beside you.

Summary

In this chapter we have noted that the way this group of cohesive ties worked was not anaphoric as with the previous groups, but by more direct linkages. The four types of conjunctions (additive, adversative, causal, and temporal), by connecting pairs of sentences, make the meaning of the text explicit. We examined a few examples from classroom reading material, and observed the nature and importance of the perception of conjunctions comprised of more than one word for the development of fluent reading. Information from research into the development of the understanding of conjunctions or connectives indicates that children up to the age of twelve have difficulty in explaining the work of connectives and that the use of the conjunction may not reflect true understanding of the semantic relations involved. It was suggested that children can be alerted to these features by a suitable classroom activity like the gap technique.

7 Lexical cohesion

There is considerable difference between lexical cohesion and the other groups of cohesive ties. Reference, substitution and ellipsis are grammatical in essence but lexical cohesion is to do with vocabulary and its selection by the speaker or author.

The term lexical derives from lexis, the technical linguistic term given to an item from the vocabulary, or lexicon of a language. You could think of it as being almost equivalent to an entry in a dictionary.

Studies of lexis and the lexicon usually involve the meaning of words and their relationships to each other in our language system.

The main relationships are synonymy, antonymy and hyponymy. Words that have the same, or nearly the same meaning, such as 'help': 'aid'; 'marsh': 'bog' are said to be synonyms. Words that are opposite or nearly opposite in meaning like 'neat': 'untidy'; 'quick': 'slow' are termed antonyms. The other relationship, that of hyponymy, involves inclusion of a more specific term within a general one. The word 'tree' for instance, has as its hyponyms, 'oak', 'ash', 'fir', 'chestnut', 'sycamore' etc. We often define words using this relationship (e.g. a robin is a kind of bird or a trout is a kind of fish). (See Chapman et al., 1979) for a discussion of word meaning with some useful classroom activities.)

We find, as we did with other cohesive ties, that those categorised as achieving cohesion through lexical or word association aspects can also be sub-divided into groups, in this case, reiteration and collocation.

Reiteration

We find in certain texts that the same word is repeated to a greater or lesser extent and that this repetition creates cohesion. Look at the extent of repetition in the following passage for instance:

> He asked his tall aunt, the Ostrich, why her tail feathers grew so, and his tall aunt the Ostrich spanked him with her hard, hard claw. He asked his tall uncle, the Giraffe, what made his skin spotty, and his tall

uncle, the Giraffe, spanked him, with his hard, hard hoof. And still he was full of 'satiable curiosity'. *He asked* his broad aunt, the Hippopotamus why her eyes were red, and his broad aunt, the Hippopotamus, spanked him with her broad, broad hoof; and *he asked* his hairy uncle the Baboon, why melons tasted just so, and his hairy uncle, the Baboon, spanked him with his hairy, hairy paw. And still he was full of 'satiable curiosity'. *He asked* questions about everything that he saw, or heard, or felt, or smelt or touched, and all his uncles and his aunts spanked him. And still he was full of 'satiable curiosity'.

(From *Just So Stories* by Rudyard Kipling (1902) Macmillan)

In the extract we have emphasised *he asked* only from many other instances of reiteration. There are many other similar examples of lexical cohesion in the passage, 'spanked him' for example: and the repetition of *'he asked'* and 'spanked him' will almost certainly receive emphasis when read aloud. In this particular instance, the reiteration is very much a characteristic of Kipling's style, but there are many other examples of less obvious reiteration. Lexical cohesion, then can be thought of as being concerned with the quality of the text, its feel or its style, as well as this cohesive characteristic.

Another type of repetition is by the relationship of synonymy (that is words having the same or nearly the same meaning). Look for example at this passage from another author:

At winter's end he returned to the Great House. He was made *sorcerer* then, and the Archmage Genster accepted at that time his fealty. Thenceforth he studied the high arts and enchantments, passing beyond arts of illusion to the works of real magery, learning what he must know to earn his *wizard's* staff.

(From *A Wizard of Earthsea* by Ursula Le Guin, op.cit.)

Here 'sorcerer' and 'wizard' are synonyms and as such are lexically cohesive.

Another reiterative device that is cohesive is the hyponym or superordinate. As already indicated, this is a term used for the general word within which is included the meaning of more specific words e.g. 'flower' is a superordinate of 'tulip' or 'daisy' or 'daffodil' etc.

In this extract you will find the near-synonyms 'sound' and 'noise' used as superordinates of 'splutter' and 'sniff'.

They stopped to listen, and suddenly they were startled by a very peculiar *sound* from the other side of the hedge; it sounded like a muffled *motor-horn*, and it ended in a *splutter*. They heard a *sniff*, then another *splutter* and the odd *honking noise*.

(From *Worzel Gummidge*, by B.E. Todd, op.cit.)

We could extend the superoridinates to cover *muffled motor horn* and *honking*.

The final reiteration type to be mentioned is the general noun, and here the process comes close to the reference type of cohesive tie discussed in Chapter 4. Halliday and Hasan (1976, p.274) put it thus: 'The class of general nouns is a small set of nouns having generalised reference within the major noun classes, those such as "human noun", "place noun", "fact noun" and the like.'

Examples given are:

people, person, man, woman, child, boy, girl (human)
creature (non-human animate)
stuff (inanimate concrete mass)
business, affair, matter (inanimate abstract)
move (action)
place (place)
question, idea (fact) (p.271 *et seq.*)

Halliday and Hasan also point out, in discussing general nouns, that:

> From a lexical point of view, they are the superordinate members of major sets of vocabulary items, and therefore, their cohesive use is an instance of the general principle whereby a superordinate item operates anaphorically as a kind of synonym. From a grammatical point of view, the combination of general noun plus specific determiner, such as *the man, the thing*, is very similar to a reference item.

We have, then, four categories of reiteration:

> (i) the same word, (ii) a synonym or near synonym, (iii) a superordinate or (iv) a general noun.

Collocation

The other major group of lexically related items consists of those that occur in collocation with one another. Words that occur together regularly are said to be collocated. This can happen in closely associated pairs like 'bread and butter' or 'mild and bitter', or in some phrases like 'all through the night', or 'stand and deliver'. You can test the strength of these associations by deleting the final words and ask children to complete them. You will find some of these collocations are more predictable than others e.g. 'Fish and_____', 'bus_____', 'cat and _____'.

This habitual association is largely independent of grammatical structures, being a relationship between lexical items and not between classes of words. The concept of collocation in lexical cohesion is given 'to any pair of lexical items that stand to each other in some recognisable lexicosemantic (word meaning) relation'. (Halliday and Hasan, 1976, p.285.) So in addition to the synonym and superordinates mentioned above, we can include opposites like 'boy' and 'girl' and 'love' and 'hate'. Included also are words that appear in series, like the days of the week, and points of the compass, and other similar sets of words. 'In general, any two lexical items having similar patterns of collocation, that is tending to appear in similar contexts – will generate a cohesive force.' (Halliday and Hasan, 1976, p.286.) These incidences can build up into long cohesive chains and word patterns.

In the following examples the words forming chains have been italicised:

> 'let's start at once', said Roger, but at that moment the *kettle* changed its tune. It had been *bubbling* for some time, but now it *hissed* quietly and steadily, and a long *jet* of *steam* poured from its *spout*. The *water* was *boiling*. Susan took the *kettle* from the fire, and emptied into it a small packet of tea.
>
> (From *Swallows and Amazons* by Arthur Ransome, op.cit.)

Here, 'kettle . . . bubbling . . . hissed . . . jet of steam . . . spout . . . water . . .boiling . . . provide an example of the cohesive effect of a chain of collocates. Other examples can be found readily as in:

> The whale-backed *Pennines*, in their southern *reaches*, crumble into separate *hills* which join up with the Staffordshire *moors*, and form the Cheshire *plain*. Two *hills* stand out above all the rest. One is Bosley Cloud, its north *face* sheer, and southwards a graceful sweep to the *feet* of the Old Man of Mow, but, for all that, a brooding, sinister *mountain*, forever changing shape when seen from meandering Cheshire lanes. The other is Shuttlingslow. It is a *cone* in outline, but with the top of the *cone* sliced off, leaving a flat, narrow exposed *ridge* for a *summit*. And three days hence, on that *ridge*, eight miles from where they now were, Firefrost would be given into safe hands – if the northbrood could be kept at bay for so long.
>
> (From *The Weirdstone of Brisingamen* by Alan Garner, op.cit.)

Here, as in the other passages quoted, the chain of words 'Pennines .
.. hills ... moors ... plain ... face ... feet ... mountain ... cone ...
ridge ... summit' has within it reiteration and other cohesive ties.
The words 'hill' and 'ridge' are repeated and there are other two- and
three- word collocations like 'brooding, sinister', 'southern ...
north ... southwards' and phrases like 'for all that', 'all the rest'. It is
noticeable that the cohesive effect extends not only across sentences
but is inevitably involved with the mood or theme of the text.

Lexical cohesion and anticipation

In discussing lexical cohesion I have mentioned the associations
that are built up between words. Word association is, of course, a
well-known concept in psychology, and is important when we view
reading from a psychological perspective as well as this mainly text
linguistic approach. As remarked earlier, a good deal of the skill of
fluent readers comes from their ability to anticipate, and word
associations greatly assist this process.

We have seen in lexical cohesion some of the more important of
the linguistic features that the reader may be aware of from his
overall language facility. It would come as no surprise to the teacher
developing reading to know that simple collocations such as 'for all
that', 'all the rest' and so on ('and so on' is one too!) will be read
competently once the collocation has been anticipated and confirmed.
Furthermore, it may not have escaped notice that some of the other
cohesive ties, eg 'at first' the conjunction, have a collocational effect
from being a small group of words that regularly co-occur. However,
some of the other relationships that are strung out throughout a
passage as though on a chain, are not so easily appreciated until
underlying semantic awareness has developed. It is this extended
use of the concept of collocation to cover associations through a
passage that is a major contribution to our appreciation of cohesion
in texts.

Semantic fields

Many of the lexical groups of words we have been discussing fall
into what are called semantic or lexical fields. These are groupings
of words that are closely associated around a concept or a central
idea. The kinship group of words is a well-known example: mother,
father, son, daughter, grandmother, grandfather, cousin, uncle and
aunt. This particular semantic field is a closed set of words which

have obvious relationships to do with kinship. Another field which has been explored is the semantic field of colour names which make up the colour spectrum. Look at the following diagram which is taken from Fillenbaum and Rapoport (1971, p.53). This shows the semantic field (or domain) of colour names arranged in what is called 'a two-dimensional Euclidean representation'. The notion behind this is that meaning can be thought of as occupying semantic space in which the meaning of one item in a semantic field can be envisaged as being in closer proximity to some items in the same field than others, albeit they are all concerned with a similar basic concept. In the diagrams in Figure 9, while all the items are colour names, red is judged by the students as being closer to scarlet in meaning than it is to orange, whereas orange is seen to be nearer to yellow than pink.

The investigators base their research on the assumption that 'the meaning of a lexical item is a function of the set of meaning relations

Figure 9. Semantic field of colour names

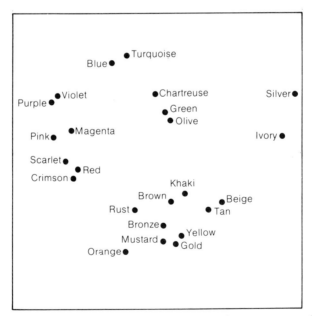

Two-dimensional Euclidean representation for a group of 17 male university students' judgments

which hold between that item and other items in the same domain' (page 3). To find out whether the structured relations proposed by linguists have psychological reality, they carried out a series of empirical studies with different methods of collecting the data and different ways of analysing it. The illustrations here are taken from one analysis of the results of the judgements of 17 male and 17 female university students who were asked to connect the most similar colour names together so as to construct a diagram which is called a 'labelled-tree' (page 15). You will observe how the results show that the colour names are arranged by the students in certain clusters. The red-violet cluster (crimson, red, scarlet, pink, magenta, purple, violet) is one obvious one while the orange-yellow is another. Other semantic fields examined in the same way were kinship terms, pronouns, prepositions, conjunctions, emotion words, have verbs, verbs of judging and good-bad terms. Reviewing their work, the authors claim that their results support the main contention

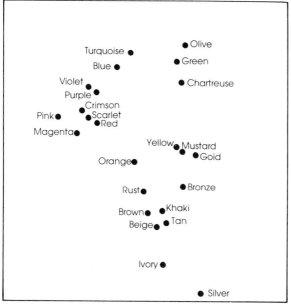

Two-dimensional Euclidean representation for a group of 17 female university students' judgments

(After Fillenbaum and Rapoport, 1971)

that 'meaning should be treated as a function of meaning relations, that the notion of semantic structure be defined "in terms of certain relations that hold between the items of a particular sub-system".' If you are considering working with these concepts with children you should note that Fillenbaum and Rapoport found that working with emotion names and evaluative terms produced disappointing results, at least, that is, with their methodology.

There are many other semantic fields which reveal some intersting inter-relationships of words. Take, for example, the semantic field of cooking terms: 'cook', 'bake', 'fry', 'roast', 'simmer', etc. The terms are familiar enough in everyday life, and while children will be aware that each of the terms is to do with cooking, it will be some time before they differentiate between them. We should not be misled into thinking, however, that the experiences that will assist word meaning development will occur efficiently without the attention of teachers. Children sometimes find it difficult to distinguish between meanings which are closely related. A useful activity to assist them is to provide a setting within which they can attempt the differentiations involved. For example, a matrix is arranged as in Figure 10 and the unique characteristics of some lexical items more clearly revealed (see Lehrer, 1974, for some interesting semantic fields for children to explore).

Figure 10. Matrix for distinguishing the meaning of closely related 'cooking terms'

Cooking terms

Food items	boiling	roasting	baking	frying	braising	other
meat	✓ ?	✓	✓ ?	✓	✓	
eggs	✓	x	✓ ?	✓	?	
cake	?	x	✓	x	x	
fish	✓	?	✓	✓	x	
cabbage	✓	x	x	?	x	
potatoes	✓	✓	✓	✓	✓	
ice-cream	x	x	x	x	x	
other						

Take the extent of another set of words within the semantic field of sound words, for example – racket, clamour, rattle, clatter, crash, shrill, screech, strident, din, deafening and ear-splitting. These and the subsets of the field include 'snap, crackle, pop' and ring, chime, clang, toll, trill'. They could be investigated by groups of children in a similar way.

One interesting feature of the research mentioned earlier into the development of semantic fields (Chapman, 1975) was the way in which children responded in terms of opposites when asked for similarities. Adults would relate 'he and his' and 'she and her' as being most similar while the children would put 'he and shc' and 'boy and girl'. The adult would relate along the sex dimension but children would relate along another i.e. age: boy and girl; man and woman; grandmother and grandfather. It is as though children preferred the primary word association of oppositeness. The same was true with the colour words where, instead of relating words along hues (red, pink, etc.) as did adults, the children saw, for example, black and white as being more closely connected than other combinations. This effect of putting opposites as close or near in meaning continues spasmodically, while the strength of other associations is growing, until the eleven/twelve year age-groups.

We have noted that problems surround the acquisition of words like 'similar' and 'like x' (Karmiloff-Smith, 1977) and it could be thought that this was affecting the outcome of the tasks put before the children. This may have played a part, particularly among the six-year-olds but it is unlikely to account for the consistency of the results throughout. The analysis showed that children were still attaining mastery of the semantic organisation of words into such lexical organisations as semantic fields well into the middle-school age-group.

As well as these experimental tasks concerning semantic fields, certain investigations were carried out to try to find out how children remembered items which had various semantic relationships, such as opposites, the superordinates (eg. flower: tulip, daffodil, daisy, etc.) and synonyms. It was found that up to eleven years of age words of the same frequency of occurrence in the vocabulary of children being tested were recalled as opposites more readily than they were as superordinates or synonyms.

These results illustrate the point that language is continuing to develop in many ways that may not be readily apparent. This language development needs to be encouraged if the demands made on reading by the curriculum are to be met.

If these research results have any implications for reading instruction (and they do, of course, require much more detailed study), the major one is to bring the underlying semantic relationships that exist between words to the notice of children to help them as their language skills develop. So alerted, pupils will be able to recognise such relationships and anticipate them in their reading.

Summary

We have seen that cohesion can be achieved through the author's choice of vocabulary and that this type of cohesion, lexical cohesion, occurs in two important forms. Reiteration (the repetition of words, including the same word, a synonym or near synonym, a superordinate or a general noun) was the first to be examined and exemplified. The second, collocation, was illustrated and attention was drawn to its affinity to the psychological process of word association.

Using the concept of semantic fields, it was suggested that the sense of words (their meaning relationships) took time to develop, but was another important factor in language development and teaching.

8 Cloze procedure

Cloze procedure has become a familiar subject among reading specialists but for any reader who has not worked with it, I will give a brief introduction and draw attention to the considerable amount of writing and research that has been undertaken in cloze since its inception. From even this short account teachers may be able to construct many varied practical activities to suit the level of their pupils' reading. (A useful annotated bibliography has been produced for the International Reading Association by McKenna and Robinson, 1980.)

Introduction to cloze

Taylor (1953) introduced this technique for measuring communication by deleting certain words from a text when he was a graduate student at the University of Illinois. The technique derives its name from the Gestalt concept of 'Closure' which is concerned with the tendency we have to complete a structural whole by 'filling gaps' during perception. (For a summary of Gestalt psychology see Chaplin and Krawiec, 1968.)

The standard example given by Gestalt psychologists is that of an incomplete circle. When shown to subjects under experimental conditions they tend to perceive the circle as a whole; that is, they mentally fill the gaps. It was suggested by Taylor that if words were deleted from a text, the reader, when presented with such a mutilated version, would mentally 'close the gap' and replace the deleted words. These words would match the author's intended meaning.

This explanation of the title 'cloze' has been the generally accepted explanation of the procedure. However, Weaver (Kingston, 1977) pointed out that there was a second rationale for the procedure and, what is more, a less trivial one than that of 'closure'. The other rationale was derived from the so-called 'information theory' of the communication engineers. He suggests that, 'the term "cloze" and the closure explanation is misleading as a designation of this procedure because it arouses in the thinker the more common constructs of Gestalt psychology which have always been difficult to apply to verbal situation'. Attention is also drawn by Kingston to Rankin's (1957) exhaustive review of cloze where cognitive aspects are regarded as more important than the perceptual. From these findings Weaver argues that it is preferable to think of cloze as a recoding operation. In this way, the explanations of information theorists could be used to help researchers and others understand how cloze works.

The technique, in message transmission terms, was seen as intercepting the author's message (the text), mutilating it by deletions, and then requiring message receivers to reconstruct the original. From the replacements made by the receivers who try to make the language patterns whole, we can get a general measure of the passage's readability; that is, how difficult or easy the passage is to read.

One of the concepts that has come from the information theorists and which helps in our understanding of cloze, is that of redundancy. And here we should point out that the term 'information' is used in a special way. For the information theorist, information is quantifiable as 'reduction of uncertainty', or to put it another way, the more information there is the less uncertainty there is. This has applications to fluent reading, for the more information there is in a passage the easier it will be to predict what is to come.

Horning (1979), in her attempts to find an operational definition of redundancy, brings together Smith's and Goodman's definitions thus:

> Redundancy exists whenever information is duplicated by more than one source, and, in the case of reading, information is duplicated by at least four sources or even systems. Redundancy, or the use of it, is crucial to proficient reading, but is at the same time largely unconscious.

For our purposes, the operational definition Horning puts forward is of interest in that it spells out some of the cohesive ties we have been investigating. She begins with syntax, suggesting the re-arrangement of sentences that are embedded, thus

> replace pronouns with their referents; add a referent to any unclear 'this'; replace dummy subjects such as 'it' and 'there' with real subjects in any sentence or clause; and finally change passives to actives. In making changes in a text, a researcher must exercise some judgement; changes which produce nonsensical or awkward phrasing should not be made.

Of semantic redundancy she suggests that it might be operationally defined as

> additions to the text in the following forms: the addition of examples in phrases beginning with 'for example' or 'for instance'; the addition of specification of particulars, in phrases beginning with 'such as'; or the clarification of term or concept . . .

From the reading teacher's viewpoint these are useful, practical ways of making texts easier to read. Some might suggest that to increase redundancy in this way might make the text boring and here the teacher's judgement must be used, for if it was difficult to begin with, it would be both boring and frustrating.

Another very important point needs emphasis here before you go ahead to construct your own materials. You will have noticed in the first quote above from Horning that 'information is duplicated by at least four sources or cue systems'. If, then, we use various cues to predict what is to come in reading, then when a pupil is replacing a word in a cloze text we should be very careful how we interpret the results or, as noted in relation to pronouns, to decide how the child produced the missing word. You may have intended your cloze passage, for example, to act as a teaching device that alerted your pupils to the use of certain cohesive ties. The actual replacement of a specific word in the cloze passage, however, is the result of many cues acting together. In other words, the child might have got a word that fits, even the author's word, by a combination of cues, basically graphophonemic, syntactic (within the sentence) and cohesive, (across sentences). When one end of a cohesive tie is deleted, however, as its identity comes from outside the structure of the sentence containing the deletion, the dominant cue is a cohesive one. The best method is probably to ask children to replace the words and then tell you or their fellow pupils in group work how they arrived at their choice. In this way you will have a much more reliable idea of the predominant cueing systems at work for individual readers in any particular text. This method also supplies many opportunities for direct teaching.

Cloze as a measuring instrument

A useful outline of how to carry out cloze procedure to discover readability levels was given by Potter (1968), who suggests that the most valid and reliable cloze text for measuring passage difficulty is one in which:

(1) An every nth mechanical mutilation system is used.
(2) Not more than 20 words out of every hundred are deleted.
(3) Passage length is at least 250 words.
(4) Deletion ratios of 1:10 and 1:12 in longer passages may be valid for certain purposes.
(5) At least 50 words are deleted in order to ensure adequate sampling of passages.
(6) The exact word deleted is indicated as the most useful and efficient scoring criterion.
(7) Other scoring systems (synonym, form class) provide less inter-scorer reliability and require substantially more time.
(8) The separate scoring of form classes or content and function words may provide specific information for specialised purposes.

This procedure gives a useful measure of the readability of any particular passage. In case the process is unfamiliar, by 'nth mechanical mutilation' Potter means that, after you have made the first deletion, every fifth, tenth, or twelfth word is then deleted whatever that word is. The first paragraph, or hundred words, should be left intact to allow the reader to establish a context for the passage.

Much research has been done to test the validity of the procedure in relation to readability. Most of this research, with minor modification, supports the initial findings, which were that 'the cloze procedure ranks passages at differing difficulty levels in the same order as do older readability formulas' (Potter, 1968).

In the same report's summaries of the nature of cloze, we should also note that Taylor (1957) is reported as suggesting that 'pairs of words that have a high or a low probability of occurring together, greatly influence cloze scores. The most frequent sequential associations (e.g. bread and butter; bus stop; home and dry) would tend to limit the population of possible cloze responses.' I drew attention to this point in Chapter 7, where the process of association within the lexical cohesion group of cohesive ties was discussed. Teachers wishing to construct cloze exercises should take this into account, therefore, along with comment (8) above of Potter's summary.

Bickley et al. (1970) wrote an article which brought together much of the research on cloze up until that time, thus providing 'a quick reference conspectus of the research', to which the reader's attention is drawn for further study.

We have looked very briefly at some of the earlier research into cloze procedure as a measuring instrument for the readability level of passages, and should note that the technique has been used in the same way as a measure of comprehension. I now turn to its application in the field of children learning English as a second or foreign language.

Cloze in second language learning

Anderson (1976) carried out a series of ten experiments using the cloze procedure with second language learners. His evaluation of cloze followed Osgood's six criteria for evaluating measuring instruments. These are objectivity, reliability, validity, sensitivity, comparability, and utility. I follow Anderson's evaluation because it gives a useful check-list for the validity and reliability of cloze tests when they are prepared by teachers for classroom use.

Firstly, Anderson evaluated cloze 'as a measure of both the readability of written language and the ability of subjects to comprehend written language'. He records this as follows: 'The procedure for obtaining cloze scores was not influenced in any way by the investigator and this is the essence of objectivity.' He found next that it was a valid instrument for both reading difficulty and reading comprehension. As to sensitivity (implying both reliability and validity), he states that cloze procedure is sensitive to the degree that it discriminates between the reading difficulties of passages and between the reading comprehension abilities of subjects. His evidence showed that it 'reflected as fine distinctions in reading comprehension as are ordinarily made by traditional comprehension measures'. The same positive evaluation was true of comparability (ie. the extent to which it can be applied to a wide variety of situations), and to its utility.

While acknowledging that more research is necessary to replicate so as to confirm, or otherwise, his results, Anderson states that 'cloze procedure may be used to measure the reading difficulty of English for second language learners' and also that 'cloze procedure may be used to measure the reading comprehension abilities of non-native speakers learning English'.

There are, as Anderson points out, many problems yet to be resolved, but cloze procedure does appear to be potentially useful in other parts of the world where English is learned as a second or foreign language and, one would imagine, for children learning English in Britain, Australia, etc. whose mother tongue is not English.

Cloze as a teaching technique

In addition to its use as a measuring instrument for assessing passage readability and children's comprehension in both first and second language, cloze has also been recommended as a useful teaching technique (see Jongsma 1971, 1980; Bortnick and Lopardo 1973; Gunn, 1978; Gunn and Elkins, 1979). The last-named authors make some interesting points to help teachers exploit the techniques so as to extend children's reading. This involves the teacher constructing texts in such a way as to involve the pupil in active learning. They warn that if care is not taken, cloze exercises might not involve active participation to a degree that will achieve progress. 'For instance, the dog wagged his _____, requires only a low level of conscious processing for solution.' Contrast this with the more active deeper-level type taken from Elkins and Andrews (1974), involving elementary problem solving skills: 'Their island is so _____ you can walk around it in a few _____.' It is interesting to note in passing that Gunn and Elkins (1979) also speak of conscious awareness.

We have alluded to this feature in Chapter 3 where we noted that children gradually become aware of language as a phenomenon in its own right, apart from its functional aspects. It is suggested that the use of the cloze procedure can heighten children's awareness of language from what is presumably an *unconscious* level or tacit awareness to the *conscious* level of active awareness. Gunn and Elkins put the practical outcome thus:

> In order to talk about their choice of words, children must not only be aware of the appropriate reasons for choosing a response but they must be able to explain their reasons to others, and, if necessary, defend their choice.

If you have followed the approach to reading in this book so far, you will appreciate that children's ability to be consciously aware of their language, in order to perform the types of work recommended needs some such element as linguistic awareness. It is particularly useful for working in groups where we would expect pupils to become more able to 'comment' on their own language and at the same time, as Bruner puts it, 'go beyond the information given' (Bruner, 1973). These active learning processes involve bringing children's working language into focus so that they can appreciate its potential more fully. Cloze procedure does this in a variety of ways, some of which we can now look at.

Mention is made by Gunn and Elkins (op.cit.) of context cues and it is suggested that the cloze procedure can assist teachers to use them in a systematic fashion. They also show how, at (Australian) Year 3 level (i.e. children of about nine years of age), teachers can give a series of exercises to encourage word attack skills and vocabulary development. In the former they show how cloze procedure can be used to enhance children's ability to anticipate during reading, initially through the use of highly predictable sequences like nursery rhymes and familiar expressions.

Gunn and Elkins (op.cit.) recommend the practice of reading the mutilated text right through before starting to complete the deletions (Bortnick and Lopardo, 1973). This encourages the reader to take account of context cues that are not in the immediate environment of the deletion. They illustrate this by drawing attention to the first word missing in the following story:

One day, Peter saw a _____ in the window of the hobby shop. Peter _____ a very determined boy and would _____ anything to get what he _____. He really wanted this boat.

It might be helpful to teachers new to cloze procedure, to quote Bortnick's and Lopardo's directions to pupils working on cloze texts. They suggest:

- Read through the entire cloze passage silently.
- Reread the cloze passage, writing in words you think fit the blanks.
- If you can, try to offer your reasons for your choices for these blanks (teacher selects certain items). 'It sound right' is a good reason in many cases.
- Compare your choices with the original passage.
- Be prepared to discuss both passages.

The authors then go on to give various uses so as 'to focus on different aspects of reading instruction'. The examples given obviously apply to different stages of reading, but teachers of most age-groups will find some that are directly applicable. The aspects mentioned were:

● Prepare cloze passages deleting certain lexical items (nouns, verbs, adjectives) to focus instruction on the syntactic constraints of the language.

● Prepare cloze passages deleting parts of words (for instance, delete all of the word except for initial and final phoneme, inflectional ending, or prefix) to focus instruction on word analysis strategies.

● Prepare cloze passages with only the first and last word of a sentence deleted as another means of focussing instruction on the syntactic constraints of the language.

● Prepare cloze passages deleting items for which students must supply synonyms to focus instruction on vocabulary (meaning development).

● Prepare cloze passages over different context areas or authors to follow instruction on differences in language structure or style.

● Prepare cloze passages in which items containing certain phoneme-grapheme correspondences are deleted (for instance all words deleted contain the short a vowel sound, consonant cluster dr, or whatever) to focus instruction on this particular type of word analysis strategy.

Vocabulary development can be very usefully enhanced also by first using simple cloze passages leading to much more challenging material. The following passage introducing the word *luminous* is given by Gunn and Elkins as an illustration:

So Becky coated paper _____ a special luminous paint. If she put the painted paper _____ a lamp, it would trap the light. The paper glowed for hours and Becky was _____ to write in the dark.

Checking the effectiveness of this, the author reported that 19 out of 60 children were able to give the correct meaning after but not before reading the cloze story, and one child responded with what is almost an unsolicited testimonial:

At thirts I thout it ment dark now I know it means light

Prediction operates at the centre of most language activity so the use of predictability cannot, therefore, be seen as being equal to guessing. Holdaway (1979) suggested an 'easier to harder continuum' in cloze for remedial teaching purpose:

1. Make few omissions, something like 1 in 120 words rather than 1 in 20, or 1 in 5 for testing.

2. Do not standardise the length of deletion line, but *do* make it the

length of the missing word.
3. Include graphic information.
4. Arrange gaps at end rather than the beginning of sentences.
5. Make language and content as close to the familiar and that of children's experience as possible.
6. Use book experience.
7. Use memorable material for impact.

These skills can then be developed so as to engage the children in making predictions about missing information in passages of increasing difficulty.

Baleyeat and Norman (1975) applied a modified form of cloze procedure to the writings of children being taught by a language experience approach (LEA). This LEA cloze test gave an easily administered and quickly scored comprehension test. The cloze format was constructed by first identifying the nouns, main verbs and adjectives, then deleting every fifth word that was one of these parts of speech. These five words were paired with distractor words of the same grammatical class and the resulting ten words were listed in random order, just after the line in which the fifth deletion had been made. The children's task was to select the correct word. As the passages had been originally written or dictated to the teacher by the children, the LEA-cloze text is a further useful variation. As a test rather than a teaching procedure, it was found to have a 'considerable positive correlation' with other achievement tests. It was especially strong on the scores of the lower age groups. It could be used also as a teaching technique and the choice of word discussed alongside the distractor.

Another type of activity is worth bringing to the attention of teachers. Although not strictly cloze procedure, it is mentioned here because it has something in common with the LEA-cloze mentioned above. This is the Maze Procedure, which has the advantage of easy construction, employing the now familiar multiple-choice technique. Indeed, it has been shown that teachers are 'able to prepare reliable, congruent maze tests of comparable difficulty if they properly follow the directions provided'. Bradley, Ackerson, and Ames (1978) state that:

A maze test may be based upon a passage sampled from any book which contains a running text, i.e., a basal (a reader from a basic reading scheme), a novel, a textbook, etc. The suggested length for a maze procedure test passage is 140 to 160 words, with every nth word a test item utilising a multiple option format. Each maze item consists of three suggested options: (a) the correct word, (b) a syntactically incorrect word, and (c) a syntactically correct but semantically incorrect word.

The authors give the following as an example:

	pole		ran	
The girl had a fishing	big.	She carried an old tin		can filled with
	apple		smart	

juicy		worms	
big cloud	worms. She tripped and	told	in the stream.
singing		fell	

They suggest, following Guthrie et al. (1974), that maze tests are easy to construct and can be administered to a group in ten to fifteen minutes. Here we are more interested in their teaching than their test potential but it is relevant to report the suggestion that several maze tests given over a period of a few weeks can be used to determine a student's instructional reading level.

Work with cloze texts is suitable for much older pupils, especially in group situations where discussion can be valuable in extending vocabulary and other language features. The reader's attention is also drawn to the work done by the Schools Council Project, *The Effective Use of Reading*, (Lunzer and Gardner, 1979). In the summary of the work concerned with improving reading through group discussion activities (Chapter 9), there are five different ways of presenting a written text, the first of which is by use of the cloze procedure. The list is:

1. group cloze
2. group SQ3R (that is, Survey-Question-Read-Recite-Review)
3. group sequencing
4. group prediction
5. group reading for different purposes

A further illustration from the Schools Council Project, (Lunzer and Gardner, 1979, page 236) shows two twelve-year-old girls both of average intelligence and reading ability discussing a passage before joining a class discussion with the teacher. The passage was:

I can hardly believe it's true. I'm almost exactly on my route, closer than I'd hoped to come in my wildest dreams. The southern tip of _____! On course, over two _____ ahead of schedule, the _____ still well up in _____ sky, the weather clearing! _____ circle again, fearful that _____ wake to find this _____ phantom, a mirage fading _____ mid-Atlantic mist. But _____ no question about it. _____ detail on the chart _____ its counterpart below; each _____ feature on the ground _____ its symbol on the _____.

The girls have read through the passage once to themselves and now read aloud.

A transcript of the girls' discussion follows showing how they arrive at an understanding of the passage using various cues. After these preliminary discussions in pairs, a group (six children) meet with the teachers for further discussion. The authors suggest that:

> the whole exercise shows great potential for teaching of technical vocabulary and terminology in context. Teachers may work from a class textbook, or have children tackle a summary of information about a topic taught over various stages in time. When used in the latter manner, group cloze seems an excellent revision exercise.

Eugene Jongsma (1980) has provided a second booklet on research into cloze used for instructional purposes. This provides teachers with a useful check list of the evidence produced by research up until publication of the booklet. This list is reproduced here for convenience. Summarising the conclusions that have arisen from the analysis and review of the literature, Jongsma lists the following:

1. The cloze procedure can be an effective teaching technique. However, it is no more nor no less effective than many other widely used instructional methods.

2. The cloze procedure is most effective in developing reading comprehension, or at least some of the skills involved in the comprehension process. It is least effective in improving word knowledge or vocabulary.

3. There is no evidence that cloze instruction is more effective for any particular type of material, such as narrative or expository. It can be effective with content material. Instruction in general cloze materials is more likely to transfer to specific content materials than specific training is to general reading.

4. Cloze instruction is no more effective for one age or grade level than another. There is also no evidence that cloze instruction is better suited to students reading either below, above, or on grade level.

5. Although the literature is mixed, cloze instruction is likely to be more effective when discussion is focussed on cues which signal responses and on the appropriateness of responses.

6. There is no evidence that one type of grouping arrangement is more effective than another for cloze instruction.

7. Cloze materials which are carefully sequenced as to difficulty, length, or purpose are more effective than undifferentiated exercises.

8. The quality of a cloze instruction program is more important than its length. There is no firm evidence as to the minimum amount of instruction that is needed before cloze is effective.

9. Selective deletion systems aimed at particular contextual relationships are more effective than semi-random deletion systems.

10. Although the research shows no difference between exact replacement and synonym scoring, some form of semantically acceptable scoring should probably be encouraged for instructional purposes.

11. There is no evidence that students have more favourable attitudes towards cloze instruction than they do toward other forms of instruction.

Summary

Cloze procedure now has a long history of research and application and is reported by those who have used it to be a very versatile teaching technique as well as a reliable measuring instrument.

As we begin to examine comprehending and those linguistic elements that go to create cohesion in texts, you will find the cloze procedure a useful tool for use in the classroom to alert your pupils to cohesive ties.

9. Comprehending

As a rule, all that you recognise in your mind is the one final association of meanings which seem sufficiently rewarding to be the answer – 'now I have understood that'; it is only at intervals that the strangeness of the process can be observed.

William Empson, quoted by Dillon (1978)

This final chapter is a conspectus. It attempts to extend and synthesise the main ideas from the preceding eight chapters into some provisional statements for teachers about reading. These statements must be provisional for as I remarked at the outset, this is only an introduction to an extensive topic which is embedded in an area of rapidly expanding knowledge. I hope however that each area will be stimulating enough to act as a jumping-off point for your further study.

What happens when we read?

You may recall that in Chapter 1 we spoke of the demands being made for all pupils to attain the standards of literacy once only achieved by the minority of pupils selected for grammar school education. We suggested that for this to be achieved the combined efforts of all teachers would be required, for it implies that all children, regardless of ability or background, will be able to comprehend what the curriculum demands they read. This demand is still often geared to the capability of the academically able pupils. We focus in this final chapter on the process of comprehending, for this is what teachers must facilitate during reading instruction, if they are to assist all their pupils to understand the text books and other reading matter they select for them.

We begin this summary by posing two related questions concerning the fundamentals. Why do we read? And what happens when we read? The answer to the first question must be to effect certain changes within ourselves, presumably for our betterment, by recovering the meaning of the communications of others. That is to say, we read to fulfil such purposes as seeking out new information to add to our existing store of knowledge, or changing our attitudes and understanding those of others, or experiencing the heightening of our emotions through the writings of novelists, dramatists and poets. It is worth stating the opposite here for it makes the point for schools more telling. What happens if our pupils do not or cannot read? They will presumably be the poorer cognitively, affectively or both, for it is unlikely that we can, as yet, achieve these life-long educative purposes as economically in other ways. The answer to the second related question, (what happens when we read?), however, concerns the rest of this chapter and then we only begin the answer.

Reading: a communication process

The changes that occur when we read are brought about by receiving the written messages of authors and integrating them with present knowledge. And it should be noted here, to prevent misunderstanding, that when words such as 'receiving' are used this does not indicate that the receptive process is a passive one: it is, as emphasised earlier, an active one of construction or reconstruction of messages.

Authors encode their messages into the written or printed mode of language for transmission purposes to overcome the 'here and now' of speech, thus giving their messages a more permanent form which, in turn, has other educational advantages. Transmission by print involves the beginning reader in a decoding operation which, while it is being learned, dominates and almost excludes much of the associated learning process of integrating those meanings with previous knowledge. However, during these early stages it is important, as I have pointed out elsewhere (Chapman, 1979c), 'to consider which is the most appropriate strategy to develop next according to the learner's present level of reading ability.' Nonetheless, this initial stage is only a small part of reading when seen from a wider language perspective. The re-creation of the author's meaning is of much greater significance as reading develops than just mastering letter/sound correspondences.

Readers and writers: a contract?

When considering reading in this way you might find it useful to adopt the perspective of Tierney and Lazansky (1980) who propose that readers and writers have responsibilities to each other. They suggest that there 'exists an allowability contract governing the role of writers during discourse production and readers during discourse comprehension'. In other words, writers intend to communicate and readers intend to interpret the messages of writers: a situation we take for granted in speech. Looked at in this way authors do not primarily express their own ideas in print, but rather direct others to construct similar thoughts from their own prior knowledge. The contractual agreement on the part of the writers includes, therefore, the responsibility that their written communications be relevant, sincere, and worthwhile.

Within such a contract the reader would assume that the writer 'communicates for certain purpose(s) to a certain audience'. It would be the reader's responsibility not necessarily to assume that the author's purpose in writing the text is the same as the reader's reading it. 'A contractual agreement between reader and writer is most tenable when reader and author agree the same terms.'

Comprehending as a language process

We have seen that a number of insights pertinent to reading arise from a study of natural languages as well as those from such areas as 'artificial intelligence'. The approach we have adopted follows from this and enables the study of reading to be enriched by the enormous wealth of research that has taken place in what is becoming known as text linguistics. This essentially eclectic approach emphasizes one of the aims of this book, which is to extend and enlarge the teacher's concept of reading.

Viewing reading as a basic language process allowed me to draw attention to some of these new insights. Areas of study such as intonation; register and style; theme and topic; speech acts; the development of word meanings; and the varieties of English all need to be considered and, where appropriate, allowed to inform classroom practice directly. We have noted that reading is sometimes considered to be a secondary process, speech having primacy, but we have also seen that the two are based on the same underlying language rule system. While the manifestation of that system has many variations, which may require a great deal of teaching support for adequate mastery, they are nonetheless encompassed within the notion of 'knowing your mother tongue'. We might pause here a moment to record the reading problems of children, and indeed adults, for whom English is a second or foreign language. Many of the linguistic features considered important are part of the implicit linguistic knowledge acquired in early childhood by the mother-tongue speaker. This knowledge enables us later, as adult language users, to recognise usages in speech or writing that are not acceptable in English, to quote one example. More often than not, mother-tongue speakers only become aware of this and other linguistic features when their attention is drawn to them. It will help therefore both pupils whose mother tongue is English and particularly those for whom it is a second language if teachers come to know these linguistic features so that they may make them explicit in their teaching.

Teachers already rely on their underlying language ability in their everyday work when, for example, correcting a piece of children's writing. We apply what is akin to an inner language to monitor the language as we read it. We are able to distinguish the acceptable from the non-acceptable. We say that such and such a sentence 'does not sound right', but sometimes we find it difficult to say exactly what it is that offends. We use this same facility when editing our own writing, testing out sentences and their linkages against our inner knowledge of the writing system. This underlying or implicit knowledge has been called by some 'linguistic awareness'. It needs to be fostered in school and can be achieved by training children to edit both their own and each other's work. This should increase their awareness of their language and thence transfer to their comprehending when reading.

Frames of knowledge and comprehending

We noted earlier that the study of artificial intelligence had given us some powerful insights into ways in which we understand texts. It was suggested that we store in our memory stereotyped chunks of knowledge which Minsky (1975) called 'frames'. Other terms have been used, such as 'scripts' by Schank and Abelson (1977), 'units' by Bobrow and Winograd (1977), and 'depictions' by Hayes (1977). Each views everyday knowledge from a different perspective but the term we use as an illustration is 'frame' as this points the way to how a topic might be developed during reading, being analagous to a 'scene' (see Fillmore, 1976).

One of the most apposite illustrations for teachers can be found in Charniak's (1972) thesis. In this work he demonstrates how a story is understood by matching incoming story information against the knowledge already stored in the memory. In order to program a computer to do this, that is, to 'understand', it is necessary to supply the computer's 'memory store' with details akin to what is built up in a human memory store over the years. It is not until we have to list such detail for a computer that we realise the extent of this real world knowledge. It is proposed by Fillmore (1976) that this knowledge can be organised within 'frames'. The 'restaurant and eating out', the 'railway station and travelling', 'the school and teaching', 'painting articles', are some everyday examples of this conventionalised knowledge.

Such a store of knowledge consists of related information about areas of world knowledge, what we might often term general knowledge, which is acquired through human experience in general. There are many such frames. In his thesis, Charniak (1968) refers to the notion of saving and a piggy-bank and the kind of information associated with it. For example he wrote down what we know about piggy-banks (PBs) for inclusion within a frame. The extent of the seemingly trivial information is quite surprising. His list looked like this:

PBs come in all sizes and shapes, though a preferred shape is that of a pig. Generally the size will range from larger than a doorknob, to smaller than a bread box. Generally money is kept in PBs, so when a child needs money he will often look for his PB. Usually, to get money out you need to be holding the bank, and shake it (up and down). Generally holding it upside down makes things easier. There are less known techniques, like using a knife to help get the money out. If, when shaken, there is no sound from inside, it usually means that there is no money in the bank. If there is a sound it means that something is in there, presumably money. You shake it until the money comes out. We assume that after the money comes out it is held by the person shaking, unless we are told differently. If not enough comes out you keep shaking until you either have enough money, or no more sound is made by the shaking (i.e. the bank is empty). In general the heavier the PB the more money in it. Some piggy banks have lids which can be easily removed to get the money out. Sometimes it is necessary to smash the PB to get the money out. To put money in, you need to have the money and the bank. The money is put into the slot in the bank, at which point you no longer are directly holding the money. Money is stored in PBs for safe keeping. Often the money is kept there during the process of saving in order to buy something one wants. PBs are considered toys, and hence can be owned by children. This ownership extends to the money inside. So, for example, it is considered bad form to use money in another child's PB. Also, a PB can be played with in the same way, as, say, toy soldiers, i.e. pushed around while pretending it is alive and doing something.

This is the amount of everyday information a computer needs to 'understand' even a simple story. By analogy we can say we and our pupils call on similar stores during comprehending. If our pupils, age level notwithstanding, are to comprehend the texts we provide for them, we will need to assure ourselves that a fair proportion of the words and relationships involved are part of their prior knowledge, that is, before they read the text. To help pupils to achieve this facility needs some thought before texts are presented to them. I wonder, for instance, how the PB list compares with a list you or your pupils might have written.

If you compose such a list and further lists within your subject area you may be surprised at the extent of the prior knowledge assumed by textbook authors. This applies, not only to the technical vocabulary that will be met, but also the relationships between the terms used. Much is added to our knowledge by reading the text, but unless our pupils have a threshold of prior knowledge their reading will be a frustrating experience instead of a learning one.

A useful activity arising out of this is for children to be set a variety of tasks, individual or cooperative, so that lists similar to the PB list can be collected. It does not require much ingenuity to put this into a purposeful and relevant activity, even if the format is a game.

Topics, themes and comprehending

Another of the insights we looked at in Chapter 3 was that of the theme or structure of a text. We looked at easy stories or narrative structures to see how children became accustomed to them, since a good deal of work has been done recently in working out in some detail whether story structures affect reading and memory of what is read. Story grammars (e.g. Mandler and Johnson, 1977) have been constructed delineating hierarchical categories within the structure of the story. These categories consolidate or make explicit the very simple ones mentioned in Chapter 3. In general, the events and episodes, responses and reactions, and final resolutions are seen in relationship to each other. For an overview of these grammars and of other types of text analysis and its relation to comprehension see Tierney and Mosenthal (1980) who provide a very useful introduction showing the strengths and weaknesses of certain analytic procedures applied in reading research in the USA.

Comprehending and language variation

I have tried to make it clear that, while all English dialects and registers are variations of the same underlying language system, some vary so much from an accepted norm that it can be difficult for some native speakers of English to understand them. It is important for the child's acquisition of literacy skills, therefore, that teachers learn something about the local dialect(s) of their children and appreciate the young child's dilemma in first encountering the language of the teacher and the school. Furthermore, the transition from the written language to the spoken is not only a question of deciphering the written code, but also of becoming familiar with the register of books. Later, in a similar fashion in the secondary school, problems related to the instructional register of textbooks become pronounced for some children.

Throughout schooling children are meeting and learning, without being taught, variations in language. Some of these variations are quite subtle and therefore difficult for them to detect and children not only have to get used to these registers, but must also learn which variation is appropriate to which social or school (subject) situation. They have to know, to use the example quoted earlier, that we don't normally address a head-teacher as 'mate'.

These differences, in themselves present some children with problems, the heavy demands of the curriculum, together with the organisation of secondary schools by subject, mean constant register switching. Many children are, unfortunately, not prepared for this and their progress in reading, in comprehending texts, suffers at the very time when they are expected to read to learn.

When we speak of fluent reading, we assume an unimpeded flow in reading which is born of understanding. This can only occur if pupils are able to anticipate what is to come next in the text and relate it to what has gone before. Such efficiency can only be achieved if our pupils are familiar with the different registers of instructional texts and have knowledge frames that have been built up with sufficient prior knowledge.

Cohesion, coherence and comprehending

We saw in Chapters 4-7 a series of examples from texts which involved Halliday and Hasan's notion of cohesion. We noted the fundamental linguistic relationship of reference and how it occurs. In speech especially, we saw how the actual physical situation was taken for granted by the speaker and the hearer. In such 'here and now' contexts both speakers and hearers assume from the context of the situation they are in that the identity of most referents is obvious. The identification for example of 'this one' or 'that one' is recoverable from the physical situation in which the words occur. We called this type of reference exophoric because the hearer had to find the identity of what is being referred to outside the words of the text. Although such reference is extra-linguistic it is nonetheless part of the message. This basic understanding of message construction enabled us to draw attention to how, within the written text, the reference is within the text itself. This endophoric reference is most important for the reader, who has to recover the identity of the reference by being cued from the text itself. This is a very complex and subtle process, for authors not only have to provide their readers with the situational context, in other words to provide the 'setting', but also to judge what level of background knowledge their readers might have. In doing this they draw on a considerable amount of both linguistic and world knowledge.

Cohesion can be envisaged as a property within the text itself providing cues for the reader for the integration of meaning. This property is not the same, according to some, as coherence. Unfortunately, the definition of coherence in texts is imprecise; Moe (1979), however, suggests that it is 'the orderly, systematic presentation of information'. It is furthermore, he argues, something 'the reader establishes or hopes to establish' in the process of reading a text. 'In this respect coherence may be viewed as the cognitive correlate of cohesion.'

Following this line of thought, the reader could be said to be cued in part by perceiving the cohesive ties while comprehending, thus creating text coherence. Cohesion, therefore, is a major text quality such that we might suggest that the more cohesive a text and the more the reader is aware of this, the more comprehending is assisted. There are, as we have noted, other characteristics of a text in addition to, and associated with, cohesion.

Tierney and Mosenthal (1980) suggest that cohesive analysis

'describes the patterns of the fabric of texture of a text . . .' and that . . . 'the text is the basic unit of the semantic system . . . It is a unit defined by its functional relevance.' They make a further point about the characteristics of textual cohesion which is worth noting. Referring to the association power of collocational items, they point out the involvement of affective aspects, the 'feel' of the text. Other types of structural analyses, because they are factual, dispense with cohesion as defined by Halliday and Hasan, and thus do not account for the important affective quality of texts.

Those interested in literary texts should examine the work of Gutwinski (1976), who examined the patterns of cohesive choices in texts written by Henry James and Ernest Hemingway. Gutwinski demonstrated that the two writers employ different cohesive patterns and suggested that the techniques he introduced might be developed and applied to other literary texts. According to Gutwinski, 'a relationship between a definite patterning of cohesive choices and a given literary style' might be established. He has already gone some way towards 'analysing cohesive patterns'.

Comprehending and the development of word meaning

We have noted how areas of everyday knowledge can be envisaged as being within knowledge frames and that these frames can be thought of as having abstract representations in the human memory. The notion has also been put forward that when these frames are alerted by reading certain key words, from then on the passage being read is 'understood' or comprehended within that frame of stereotyped knowledge. For example, if a shop is being entered, we apply a frame concerned with commercial dealings, expecting the person entering to be a 'buyer', and the person inside to be a 'seller'. Money will be expected to pass from one to the other and the idea of 'prices', 'cheap', 'dear' and their relationships to present-day monetary values will be involved. In this way the reader will proceed through the text being able to anticipate what is to come and noting divergencies from the expected.

Linguistic awareness and reading

We have mentioned the importance of the notion of linguistic awareness in earlier chapters. It was, in fact, the main topic at a conference that was held in Canada at the University of Victoria in 1979. At the final session the following statement was made:

It was generally agreed that the child's awareness of language behaviour is an important aspect of the process of learning to read. There is strong evidence of a relationship between children's awareness of the functions and features of spoken and written language and their success or failure in learning to read and write. Though a causal relationship between linguistic awareness and reading attainment has not yet been determined and more research is needed, it is clear that a *teacher's reading instruction can be better understood by children who are sensitive to the features of speech that are represented by the symbols of writing or print.* (my italics) More education for parents and teachers in ways of facilitating linguistic awareness was called for since they can promote or inhibit this sensitivity.

(Casey, 1979)

Comprehending: a constructive process

Remembering the restrictiveness of earlier concepts of reading, and the constructive nature of the reader's task outlined in this book, it is important to realise that children also need to be made aware that reading is an active process. They need to be taught strategies that assist the development of constructive comprehending skills. This can be illustrated by some research of Markman (1977). In this work, which was undertaken with children aged six to nine years, the researcher tried to find out how children become aware of their own comprehension failure, or how we realise we do not understand. She found that it was not until Grade 3 (that is around nine to ten years) that children became aware of the inadequacy of the material they were presented with as part of the reading investigation. Realising that you do not understand therefore may not be automatic, requiring little or no cognitive processing. In her article Markman makes some other interesting points which support the direction taken in this chapter. For instance, she points out the implications for a passive view of reading thus: 'When people take a passive approach to comprehension they may be unaware of their own failure to understand the information'. And, quoting references from work in cognitive development she notes that 'children in particular may be frequently misled into thinking that they understand material which they have, in fact, failed to compehend'. Citing other researchers she comments: 'Evidence is beginning to appear which indicates that developmental changes in prose comprehension may be a function of the extent and type of processing children engage in.' Her results support the hypothesis that 'children's initial insensitivity to their own comprehension failure is due to a relative lack of constructive processing'. Teachers clearly need to give support to the active processing of messages in reading.

Comprehending: the teacher's task

It is necessary when teaching reading within a broader framework to remember that it is subject to a lengthy developmental process and as such needs careful matching of materials to levels of skill and continuous support.

One basic method of encouraging this approach to reading is by the use of the cloze procedure and the modifications outlined in Chapter 8. The actual features that we have been outlining here together with the inventory of cohesive ties, provide the teacher with a rich source of activity material. Teachers could, for instance, take their present reading material, analyse it for the occurrence of the cohesive ties and their chaining, and by judicious deletion, make cloze-type activities. There are many ways in which such materials can be varied so as to provide individual work for children at levels that meet their needs. The type of material can be varied and the number and spacing of the deletions can be adjusted to increase or decrease the level of difficulty.

The type of cohesive ties being examined can be gone through systematically, so as to show children the various ways in which they can express themselves. For cloze has this added attraction for the teacher who is concerned with written language as well as reading. Being required to produce the word to fill the gap is a kind of half-way house between writing and reading.

We should note here that the use of the cloze procedure for these purposes is not to be thought of as a testing procedure. Working with cloze in the way suggested in Chapter 8 will concentrate on the cohesive relationship and this will be dominant, but other textual factors will be at work around the deletion as well as that within the cohesive tie.

Such work can continue well into the secondary school, and can be seen not only to be developing the growing linguistic awareness of our students, but also to be encouraging active comprehending, which is the ultimate goal of all reading instruction. And here we should recall that the use of the term comprehending is deliberate. It is an attempt to distinguish between the process and the product of reading. Comprehension is the term given to the product of reading and is usually measured by questions at the end of the passage. Comprehending, on the other hand, is what goes on when we are reading, and it is this process that is of interest to the teacher of reading for this is where the teacher can be most effective.

Bibliography

Adams M.J. and Collins A. (1979) A schema-theoretic view of reading. Technical Report 32, University of Illinois Center for the Study of Reading. Cambridge (Mass.), Bolt, Beranek and Newman Inc., ERIC document ED 142971.

Aitchison, J.A. (1978) *Linguistics*. London, Hodder and Stoughton.

Anderson J. (1976) *Psycholinguistic Experiments in Foreign Language Testing*. St. Lucia, University of Queensland Press.

Applebee A.N. (1978) *The Child's Concept of Stories*. London, The University of Chicago Press.

Baleyeat R. and Norman D. (1975) LEA – cloze comprehension test *The Reading Teacher* Vol. 28, pp. 555-60.

Barnard P.J. (1974) *Structure and Content in the Retention of Prose*. Unpublished Ph.D., University College, London.

Bates E. (1976) *Language and Context and the Acquisition of Pragmatics*. New York, Academic Press.

Berry M. (1975) *An Introduction to Systemic Linguistics I*. London, Batsford.

Berry M. (1977) *An Introduction to Systemic Linguistics II*. London, Batsford.

Bickley A.C., Ellington B.J. and Bickley R.T. (1970) The Cloze Procedure, *Journal of Reading Behaviour* 2, pp. 223-49.

Bobrow D.E. and Winograd T. (1977) A knowledge representation of language, *Cognitive Science* 1 (1), pp. 1-16.

Bolinger D. (1972) (ed.) *Intonation*. London, Penguin Books.

Bortnick R. and Lopardo G. (1973) An instructional application of the cloze procedure, *Journal of Reading* 16, pp. 296-300.

Bradley J.M., Ackerson G. and Ames W.S. (1978) The reliability of the cloze procedure, *Journal of Reading Behaviour* X (3), pp. 291-6.

Brazil D., Coulthard M. and Johns C. (1980) Discourse Intonation and Language Teaching. London, Longman.

Brook G.L. (1973) *Varieties of English*. London, MacMillan Press.

Brown R. (1958) *Words and Things.* New York, The Free Press.

Brown R. (1973) *A First Language: The Early Stages.* London, Allen and Unwin.

Bruner J.S. (1973) *Beyond the Information Given.* London. Allen and Unwin Ltd.

Bullock A. (1975) *A Language for Life.* London, H.M.S.O.

Casey C. (1979) Linguistic awareness in learning to read. *Reading Today International* VIII (4). Newark, Delaware, International Reading Association.

Chaplin J.P. and Krawiec T.S. (1968) *System and Theories of Psychology* (2nd Edition). New York, Holt, Rinehart and Winston.

Chapman L.J. (1975) *An Investigation of a Structuring Model for the Acquisition of Semantic Structures by Young Children.* Unpublished Ph.D. thesis, University of Aston in Birmingham.

Chapman L.J.(1979a) The perception of language cohesion during fluent reading. In Kolers P., Wrolstad M. and Bouma (eds.) *Processing Visible Language 1.* New York, Plenum Publishing Co. pp. 403-11.

Chapman L.J. (1979b) Pedagogical strategies for fluent reading. In Thackray D. (ed.) *Growth in Reading.* London, Ward Lock Educational, pp. 147-54.

Chapman L.J. (1979c) Cohesion in reading. Paper presented to the Australian Reading Association Conference 'Reading in the Year of the Child'.

Chapman L.J. (1979d) Confirming children's uses of cohesive ties in texts: pronouns. *The Reading Teacher.* 33 (3), pp. 317-22.

Chapman L.J. (1980a) Reading: Prospects for the eighties. Paper presented to the 5th Australian Reading Association Conference, Perth, W. Australia. In Bessell – Browne, Latham R., Reeves N. and Earcliner E. (eds.) *Reading into the 80s.* Adelaide, S. Australia, Australian Reading Association, 1-9.

Chapman L.J. (1980b) The development of the perception of textual cohesion. Paper presented at the 25th Annual Convention of the International Reading Association, St. Louis, Missouri, USA.

Chapman L.J. and Stokes A. (1980) Developmental trends in the perception of textual cohesion. In Kolers P., Wrolstad M., and Bourne H. *Processing of Visible Language 2.* New York, Plenum Publishing Co. pp. 219-26.

Chapman L.J., Twite S. and Swann J. (1979) *Words and Their Meanings*. Block 3, Open University Course, PE232 Language Development, Milton Keynes, The Open University Press.

Charney R. (1979) The comprehension of 'here' and 'now'. *Journal of Child Language* 6, pp. 69-80.

Charniak E. (1972) Towards a model of children's story comprehension. Unpublished Ph.D. thesis, Massachusetts Institute of Technology.

Chomsky N. (1957) *Syntactic Structures*. The Hague, Mouton.

Chomsky N. (1965) *Aspects of a Theory of Syntax*. Cambridge (Mass.), The M.I.T. Press.

Clark E.V. and Sengul L.J. (1978) Strategies in the acquisition of deixis. *Journal of Child Language* 5, pp. 457-76.

Clark, H.H. and Clark E.V. (1977) *The Psychology of Language*. New York, Harcourt, Brace Jovanovich.

Clark, M.M. (1977) *Young Fluent Readers*. London, Heinemann Educational Books.

Cruttenden A. (1974) An experiment involving comprehension of intonation in children from 7 to 10. *Journal of Child Language*. 1 (2), pp. 221-32.

Cruttenden A. (1979) *Language in Infancy and Childhood*. Manchester, Manchester University Press.

Crystal D. (1975) Neglected linguistic principles in the study of reading. In Moyle D. (ed.) *Reading: What of the Future?* London, Ward Lock Educational, pp. 26-34

Czerniewska P. (1979) *Understanding Speech*. Block 1, Open University Course, PE232 Language Development, Milton Keynes, The Open University Press.

Dillon .E.L. (1978) *Language Processing and the Reading of Literature*. Bloomington and London, Indiana University Press.

Donaldson M. (1978) *Children's Minds*. Glasgow, Fontana/Collins.

Downing J. (1976) The reading instruction register. *Language Arts* 53, pp. 762-6, 780.

Downing J. (1979) *Reading and Reasoning*. Edinburgh, Chambers.

Elkins J. and Andrews R.J. (1974) *Reading Comprehension Test*. Brisbane, Teaching and Testing Resources.

Fagan W.T. (1971/72) Transformations and comprehension. The

Reading Teacher 25, pp. 169-72.

Ferreiro E. (1978) What is written in a written sentence? A developmental answer. *Journal of Education.* Boston University, Nov. 1978.

Fillenbaum S. and Rapoport A. (1971) *Structures in the Subjective Lexicon.* London and New York. The Academic Press.

Fillmore C.J. (1976) Frame semantics and the nature of language. *Annals of the New York Academy of Science* 280, pp. 20-32.

Fletcher P. (1979) *Grammar and Grammars.* OU Course PE232, Language Development, Supplementary Material, Milton Keynes, The Open University.

Gleason H. (1969) *An Introduction to Descriptive Linguistics,* (Revised Edition). New York, Holt, Rinehart and Winston.

Gordon J.C.B. (1979) Who counts as a linguist? *UEA Papers in Linguistics* 9 pp. 11-20. Norwich, University of East Anglia.

Gregory M. and Carroll S. (1978) *Language and situation: language varieties and their social contexts.* London, Routledge and Kegan Paul.

Grimes J.E. (1975) *The Thread of Discourse.* The Hague, Mouton.

Gunn V.P. (1978) 'Blankety Blanks' for juniors. In Page G., Elkins J. and O'Connor B. (eds.) *Communication through Reading.* 1. *Focus on Comprehension.* pp.69-77. Adelaide, Australia Reading Association.

Gunn V.P. and Elkins J. (1979) Clozing the reading gap. *Australian Journal of Reading* 2 (3), pp. 144-51.

Guthrie J.T., Seifert M., Burham N.A. and Coplan R.I. (1974) The maze technique to assess, monitor reading comprehension. *The Reading Teacher* 28, pp. 161-8.

Gutwinski W. (1976) *Cohesion in Literary Texts.* The Hague, Mouton.

Halliday M.A.K. (1975) *Learning How to Mean.* London, Edward Arnold.

Halliday M.A.K. and Hasan R. (1976) *Cohesion in English.* London, Longman.

Halliday M.A.K. (1978a) Differences between spoken and written language: Some implications for literacy teaching. In Page G., Elkins J. and O'Connor B. (eds.). *Communication Through*

Reading Vol. 2. *Diverse Needs: Creative Approaches.* Proceedings of 4th Australian Reading Association Conference, Brisbane, Adelaide, Australia.

Halliday M.A.K. (1978b) *Language as Social Semiotic.* London, Arnold.

Hayes P.J. (1977) Some association-based techniques for lexical disambiguation by machine. *T.R. 25* Computer Science Department, The University of Rochester.

Hendricks W.O. (1976) Style and Discourse Analysis. In Hendricks W.O. and Van Dijk T.A. *Grammar and Styles of Grammar* (Vol. 3). Amsterdam, North-Holland Publishing Co.

Holdaway D. (1979) En-clozed. The secure prevention and remedial programme. Paper given at the 5th Australian Reading Association Conference. Perth, W. Australia.

Horning A.S. (1979) On defining redundancy in language: case notes. *Journal of Reading 22,* pp. 312-20.

Howard P. (1980) Languages of the tribe. Review of the State of the Language by Michaels and Ricks (1979). London, *The Times, 24* January 1980.

Huxley R. (1970) The development of the correct use of subject personal pronouns in two children. In Flores d'Arcais G.B. and Levelt W.J.M. (eds.) *Advances in Psycholinguistics.* Amsterdam, North-Holland Publishing Co.

Hymes D. (1971) *On Communicative Competence.* Philadelphia, University of Pennsylvania Press.

Jansen M., Jacobsen B. and Jensen P.E. (1978) *The Teaching of Reading – without really any method.* Copenhagen, Munksgaards.

Johns J.L. (1979) Beginning reading; fusing research and instruction. *Australian Journal of Reading 2* (4) 197-204.

Jongsma E. (1971) *The Cloze Procedure as a Teaching Technique.* Newark Delaware, International Reading Association.

Jongsma E. (1980) *Cloze Instruction Research: a second look.* Newark, Delaware, International Reading Association.

Joos M. (1961) *The Five Clocks.* New York, Harcourt, Bruce and World Inc.

Karmiloff-Smith A. (1976) *Little Words mean a lot: the Pluri-functionality of Determiners in Child Language.* Unpublished

Ph.D. thesis, University of Geneva.

Karmiloff-Smith A. (1977) More about the same: children's understanding of post-articles. *Journal of Child Language* 4, pp. 377-94.

Katz E.W. and Brent S.B. (1968) Understanding connectives. *Journal of Verbal Learning and Verbal Behaviour* 7, pp. 501-9.

Kingston A.J. (1977) (ed.) *Toward a Psychology of Reading and Language.* Selected writings of Wendell W. Weaver. Athens, The University of Georgia Press.

Kress E.R. (1976) *Halliday: System and Function in Language* London, Oxford University Press

Lehrer A. (1974) *Semantic Fields and Lexical Structure.* Amsterdam, North-Holland Publishing Co.

Lock A. (1980) Language development – past, present and future. *Bulletin of the British Psychological Society* 33, pp. 5-8.

Lundberg I. (1980) Aspects of Linguistic Awareness Related to Reading. In Sinclair A., Jarvella R.S. and Levelt W.J.M. (1980).

Lunzer E. and Gardner K. (1979) *The Effective Use of Reading.* London, Heinemann Educational Books.

Lyons J. (1977) *Semantics.* Vols I and II. Cambridge, Cambridge University Press.

Mackay D., Thompson B. and Schaub P. (1978) *Breakthrough to Literacy. Teacher's Manual.* London, Longman.

McKenna M.C. and Robinson R.D. (1980) *An Introduction to Cloze Procedure* (1980 revision). Newark Delaware, The International Reading Association.

McNeill D. (1966) The creation of language. *Discovery* 27, pp. 34-8.

Mandler J.M. and Johnson N.S. (1977) Remembrance of things parsed: story structure and recall. *Cognitive Psychology* 9, pp. 111-51.

Marcel T. (1978) Unconscious reading. *Visible Language* XII (4), pp. 391-404.

Markman E.M. (1979) Realizing that you don't understand. *Child Development.* 48, pp. 986-92.

Mattingly I.E. (1972) Reading, the Linguistic Process, and Linguistic Awareness. In Kavanagh J.F. and Mattingley I.G. (eds.). *Language by Ear and Eye.* Cambridge (Mass.), The M.I.T. Press.

Mercer N. and Edwards D. (1979) *Communication and Context.* Block 4, OU Course PE232, Language Development, Milton Keynes, The Open University.

Michaels L. and Ricks C. (1979) (eds.) *The State of the Language.* London, University of California Press.

Minsky M. (1975) A framework for representing knowledge. In Winston P.H. (ed.) *The Psychology of Computer Vision,* New York, McGraw-Hill.

Moe A.J. (1979) Cohesion, coherence and the comprehension of texts. *Journal of Reading* 30 (1) pp. 16-20.

Moon C. and Wells G. (1979) The influence of home in learning to read. *Journal of Research in Reading* 2 (1), pp. 53-62.

Morris J.M. (1973) You can't teach what you don't know. In Clark M.M. and Milne A. *Reading and related skills.* London, Ward Lock Educational.

Mungo C. (1979) Education Journal of the Commission for Racial Equality, quoted in *Education* 153(22) pp.629-30

O'Connor J.D. and Arnold G.F. (1973) *Intonation of Colloquial English* (second edition) London, Longman.

O'Donnell W.R. and Todd L. (1980) *Variety in Contemporary English.* London, Allen and Unwin.

OU Course PE231 *Reading Development,* (1977) Television Programme 2, *Context, Concept and Structure,* Producer D. Seligman.

OU Course PE232 *Language Development* (1979) Milton Keynes, The Open University.

Pellowski A. (1977) *The World of Storytelling.* London, R.R. Bowber & Co.

Pennock C. (1979) Introduction. In Pennock C. (ed.) *Reading Comprehension at Four Linguistic Levels.* Newark Delaware, International Reading Association.

Perera K. (1979) *Reading and Writing.* Chapter 7. In Cruttenden (1979).

Pike K.L. (1964) *Tagmamics: Beyond the Sentence.* National Council of Teachers of English, College Composition and Communication Reprint.

Potter T.C. (1968) *A Taxonomy of Cloze Research Part I. Readability* and *Reading Comprehension*. South West Regional Laboratory for Educational Research and Development.

Quirk R., Greenbaum S., Leech G. and Svartik J. (1972) *A Grammar of Contemporary English*. London, Longman.

Rankin E.F. Jnr. (1957) *An Evaluation of the Cloze Procedure as a Technique for Measuring Reading Comprehension*. Unpublished doctoral dissertation, University of Michigan.

Resnick D.P. and Resnick L.B. (1977) The nature of literacy: an historical exploration. *Harvard Educational Review* 47 (3), pp.370-85.

Richards V. (1979) Educational Journal of the Commission for Racial Equality, quoted in *Education* 153 (22), pp. 629-30.

Richek M. (1978) Evidence for a literary dialect: speaker judgements. *Journal of Reading Behaviour* X (3), pp. 257-66.

Rozin P., Bressman B. and Toft M. (1974) Do children understand the basic relationship between speech and writing? The mow-motorcycle text. *Journal of Reading Behaviour*. VI(3), pp. 327-34.

Ryan E.B. and Semmel M.I. (1969) Reading as a constructing language process. *Reading Research Quarterly* V (1), pp. 59-83.

Salinger J.D. (1958) *The Catcher in the Rye*. London, Penguin Books.

Schank R. and Abelson R. (1979) *Scripts, Plans, Goals and Understanding*. Hillsdale N.J. and Erlbaum.

Sinclair A., Jarvella R.J., and Levett W.J.M. (1980) (eds.) *The Child's Conception of Language*. Berlin, Springer-Verlag.

Sinclair J. Mc H. and Coulthard R.M. (1975) *Towards an Analysis of Discourse*. London, O.U.P.

Sinclair de Swartz H. (1971) *Piaget's Theory and Language Acquisition*. In *Piagetian Cognitive Developmental Research and Mathematical Education*. Washington, N.C.T.M.

Smith F. (1978) *Reading*. Cambridge, Cambridge University Press.

Smith N. and Wilson D. (1979) *Modern Linguistics: The results of Chomsky's Revolution*. London, Penguin Books.

Stenning K. (1978) Anaphora as an approach to pragmatics. In Halle M., Bresnan J. and Miller G.A. *Linguistic Theory and Psychological Reality*. Cambridge (Mass.), The M.I.T. Press.

Taylor W.L. (1953) Cloze procedure: a new tool for measuring readability. *Journalism Quarterly* 30, pp. 415-33.

Taylor W.L. (1957) Cloze readability scores as indices of individual differences in comprehension and aptitude. *Journal of Applied Psychology* 41 (1), pp. 19-26.

Tierney R.J. and LaZansky J. (1980) The rights and reponsibilities of readers and writers: A contractual agreement. *Reading Education Report* 13. Centre for the Study of Reading, University of Urbana –Champaign, Champaign, Illinois.

Tierney R.J. and Mosenthall J. (1980) Discourse comprehension and production: analysing text structure and cohesion. *Technical Report No. 152*. Centre for the Study in Reading, University of Urbana – Champaign, Champaign, Illlinois.

Trudgill P. (1975) *Accent, Dialect and The School*. London, Edward Arnold.

Tuinman J.J. (1974) Determining the passage dependency of comprehension questions in five major tests. *Reading Research Quarterly* 9, pp. 206-23.

Van Dijk T.A. and Kintsch W. (1977) Cognitive psychology and discourse: recalling and summarising stories. In Dressler W. (ed.) *Current Trends in Textlinguistics*. Berlin, de Gruyter W.

Vygotsky L.S. (1962) *Thought and Language*. Cambridge (Mass.), The M.I.T. Press.

Wade B. (1979) School refusal and aspects of language. *Educational Review*. 31 (1), pp. 19-26.

Webb P.A. and Abrahamson A.A. (1976) Stages of egocentricism in children's use of 'this' and 'that': a different point of view. *Journal of Child Language*. 3, pp. 349-67.

Weir R.H. (1962) *Language in the Crib*. The Hague, Mouton.

Werlich E. (1976) *A Text Grammar of English* Heidelberg, Quelle and Meyer.

Appendix 1

Sentence Links

¹On a recent sunny afternoon in Athens workers were burrowing down some distance from the Acropolis, seeking the bedrock for the foundation of a new building. ²They were being watched by the normal complement of roadside superintendents shouting occasional words of advice. ³Suddenly, the digging stopped. ⁴Instead of bedrock, the workmen had unearthed what appeared to be large slabs of smooth limestone. ⁵The workers hastily conferred with the foreman. ⁶He telephoned the site's owner who, as required by law, notified the Antiquities Department. ⁷A quick inspection by an expert from the Antiquities Department established that this site was worth investigating. ⁸The building workers departed. ⁹A guard was posted. ¹⁰Arrangements were made for sifting through the earth of the excavation next day.

Readers Digest

Notice some simple sentence linkages:

Between:		
	1 and 2	'workers: They'
	1 and 3	'burrowing: digging'
	2 and 3	'Suddenly'
	3 and 4	'Instead of'
	4 and 5	'the workmen': 'the workers'
	5 and 6	'foreman: He'
	6 and 7	'Antiquities Department' repeated
	8	'Workers' repeated

Appendix 2

Example from experimental materials on pronouns

Once there were four little fishes. They lived in a river not far from here. They enjoyed swimming along the river-bottom. They liked chasing each other among the weeds.

One day some boys went fishing in the river with fishing nets and jam jars. The fishes were playing tag among the waterweed and so _____ did not see the net. One by one _____ were caught. The boys took _____ home in a jam jar. But the boys' mother didn't want _____ in her house. So the boys took the fishes back to _____ real home, and then went back to _____. The fishes were glad to be back in _____ river again. They had waterweed for lunch, but the boys had fish and chips for _____!

Material prepared by Julienne Ramsden.

Appendix 3

Table 5.   Summary table of conjunctive relations

	External/internal	Internal (unless otherwise specified)		
Additive	Additive, simple: Additive — and, and also Negative — nor, and . . . not Alternative — or, or else	Complex, emphatic: Additive — furthermore, in addition, besides Alternative — alternatively Complex, de-emphatic: After-thought — incidentally, by the way	Apposition: Expository — that is, I mean, in other words, thus Exemplificatory — for instance, thus	Comparison: Similar — likewise, similarly, in the same way Dissimilar — on the other hand, by contrast
Adversative	Adversative 'proper': Simple — yet, though, only Containing 'and' — but Emphatic — however, nevertheless, despite this	Contrastive: Avowal — in fact, actually, as a matter of fact Contrastive (external): Simple — but, and Emphatic — however, on the other hand, at the same time	Correction: Of meaning — instead, rather, on the contrary Of wording — at least, rather, I mean	Dismissal: Closed — in any case, in either case, whichever way it is Open-ended — in any case, anyhow, at any rate, however it is

	External/internal	Internal (unless otherwise specified)		
Causal	**Causal, general:** Simple — *so, then, hence, therefore* Emphatic — *consequently, because of this* **Causal, specific** Reason — *for this reason, on account of this* Result — *as a result, in consequence* Purpose — *for this purpose, with this in mind*	**Reversed causal:** Simple — *for, because* **Causal, specific:** Reason — *it follows, on this basis* Result — *arising out of this* Purpose — *to this end*	**Conditional (also external):** Simple — *then* Emphatic — *in that case, in such an event, that being so, under the circumstances* Generalized — *otherwise, under other circumstances* Reversed polarity	**Respective:** Direct — *in this respect, in this regard, with reference to this* Reversed polarity — *otherwise, in other respects, aside from this*
Temporal	**Temporal, simple (external only)** Sequential — *then, next, after that* Simultaneous — *just then, at the same time* Preceding — *previously, before that* **Conclusive:** Simple — *finally, at last* **Correlative forms:** Sequential — *first ... then* Conclusive — *at first ... in the end*	**Complex (external only):** Immediate — *at once, thereupon* Interrupted — *soon, after a time* Repetitive — *next time, on another occasion* Specific — *next day, an hour later* Durative — *meanwhile* Terminal — *until then* Punctiliar — *at this moment*	**Internal temporal:** Sequential — *then, next, secondly* Conclusive — *finally, in conclusion* **Correlative forms:** Sequential — *first ... next* Conclusive — *... finally*	**'Here and now':** Past — *up to now, hitherto* Present — *at this point, here* Future — *from now on, henceforward* **Summary:** Summarizing — *to sum up, in short, briefly* Resumptive — *to resume, to return to the point*

INDEX